BOB CHASE is one of the leading advocates for public education. He is the two-term president of the National Education Association, the nation's largest teachers union, and serves on the board of the National Commission on Teaching and America's Future. A former middle school teacher, Chase writes a by-lined column that appears in *The Washington Post* and *Education Week*, and he has appeared as a guest on numerous television and radio programs, including CNN's *Crossfire*, NBC's *Today Show*, ABC's *Good Morning America*, and PBS's *News Hour*.

BOB KATZ writes frequently on issues concerning parents and children. His writing has appeared in the *New York Times*, *Newsweek*, *Parents*, and numerous other publications, and he is the author of the novel *Hot Air*.

Praise for

THE NEW PUBLIC SCHOOL PARENT

"*The New Public School Parent* is an essential guide for all parents seeking meaningful ways to improve their children's educational experience. Applying a wealth of experience, Bob Chase provides extremely practical strategies that will enable parents to comfortably and effectively engage with their children's school community."
—James P. Comer, M.D., Yale University Child Study Center

"*The New Public School Parent* recognizes that parental involvement is the key to student success. Now parents have a real-life guide to navigating today's public school system."
—Shirley Igo, President, National PTA

"This book is good news for parents. Bob Chase brings an insider's insights to the often-perplexing experience of public schools—and offers innovative, on-target, practical solutions to common challenges. This work is an extremely useful tool for parents who wish to take responsibility for their children's education."
—Richard Riley, former Secretary of Education

"Considering a child annually spends 900 hours in school and 7,800 outside school, it behooves America to get its parents more involved in education. Bob Chase's book offers a wise and comprehensive blueprint for that involvement. His lifetime of experience in public schools offers an uncomplicated map to parental involvement that helps the parent, the teacher, and, most importantly, the child."
—Jim Trelease, author of *The Read-Aloud Handbook*

THE *NEW* PUBLIC SCHOOL PARENT

*How to Get
the Best Education
for Your Child*

BOB CHASE

with Bob Katz

PENGUIN BOOKS

PENGUIN BOOKS

Published by the Penguin Group

Penguin Putnam Inc., 375 Hudson Street,
New York, New York 10014, U.S.A.
Penguin Books Ltd, 80 Strand,
London WC2R 0RL, England
Penguin Books Australia Ltd, 250 Camberwell Road,
Camberwell, Victoria 3124, Australia
Penguin Books Canada Ltd, 10 Alcorn Avenue,
Toronto, Ontario, Canada M4V 3B2
Penguin Books India (P) Ltd, 11 Community Centre, Panchsheel Park,
New Delhi–110 017, India
Penguin Books (N.Z.) Ltd, Cnr Rosedale and Airborne Roads,
Albany, Auckland, New Zealand
Penguin Books (South Africa) (Pty) Ltd, 24 Sturdee Avenue,
Rosebank, Johannesburg 2196, South Africa

Penguin Books Ltd, Registered Offices:
Harmondsworth, Middlesex. England

First published in Penguin Books 2002

1   3   5   7   9   10   8   6   4   2

Copyright © Bob Chase and Bob Katz, 2002
All rights reserved

ISBN 0 14 20.0136 8

LIBRARY OF CONGRESS CATALOGING IN PUBLICATION DATA AVAILABLE

Printed in the United States of America
Set in Sabon and Tekton
Designed by M. Paul

Acknowledgments

We wish to thank the following colleagues at the National Education Association who helped this project with thoughtful insight and analysis: Ed Amundsen, Glen Cutlip, Marcella Dianda, Jim Whitmire, Carol Edwards, Connie Eskesen, Barbara Kapinus, Kate Mattos, Pamela Matthews, Patti Ralabate, Warlene Gary, Isabelle Rodriguez, Peter Arum, Brad Ritter, Becky Fleischauer, Gaye Barker, Marian Galbraith, Mark Simon, Richard Verdugo, Chuck Williams, Cynthia Miles, Deanna Duby, Barbara Stein, Bouy Te, Robert Glenn, Susan Gilman, and Kevin Teeley. We would like to extend a special thanks to Jerald Newberry and David Sheridan who gave generously of their time and expertise.

Mary Bablitch assisted with smart manuscript reviews, good ideas, and patient support. Andrew Krensky provided timely research assistance. In addition, we were fortunate to be enlightened about the intricate ways of public schools by a number of veteran educators, including Ron Axelrod, Frances Farr, Carol Franz, Alison Tyler, Dallas Rust, Lauren Foley, and Carol Stearns.

This book would not have been possible without the energetic efforts of literary agent George Greenfield, the savvy manuscript comments provided by Susan Hans O'Connor, and the guidance and encouragement of our editor, Janet Goldstein.

For

Jennifer and Ian
Heather and Wes
and Zoe, my
brilliant and beautiful
granddaughter

Table of Contents

Introduction

I am not sure where I would be if not for public schools. Growing up, I was not part of a family where education was emphasized. My mother had an eighth-grade education, my father only a high school diploma. I have five siblings, two of whom never finished high school. I am the only member of my immediate family to go on to college.

When I occasionally find myself in heady company, as, for example, at the 1999 White House Summit on the New Economy when, appointed by President Clinton, I sat on a panel alongside Bill Gates of Microsoft and the president of the World Bank, I can't help but reflect on the long road I've traveled.

And when I do so, I have no difficulty identifying the source of my good fortune.

It was not only my parents but also public schools. Public schools made all the difference for me, as they have for so many. Good teachers made the difference. Good teachers helped me understand that I was worth something, that I had the potential to be more than I could imagine. Public education has the nearly magical capacity to open up unimaginable worlds for children, as it did for me.

As I like to say, before becoming president of the NEA I had a real job. I was a middle school social studies teacher. It was as fine and fulfilling a job as I could imagine. Every day presented new challenges. Every day was a chance to excite young minds in important ways. As a teacher, you never face an existential crisis about the meaning of your work. You see it in your kids' faces. You see it in the fires you kindle in their minds. You see it in your students' gratitude when they come back to visit you years later.

I believe I was a good teacher. I certainly felt I knew what school was all about—until my daughters entered school.

Turns out, the world of education changes drastically when you're a parent. This fact rudely caught up with me when my daughter was in middle school. She was struggling in math. My daughter asked for extra help in math. The teacher initially said he was unavailable. I pressed for a meeting. The teacher suggested an early-morning visit that was not possible with my work schedule. I asked for other times. He did not respond.

Now remember, I was an experienced teacher, a leader in the state education association. I should have been on sound footing. But at first, I did not know how to react. I was totally at a loss. I had never been in this position before. Do I accept defeat? Do I take a stand? What are my rights? What are my daughter's? And it struck me, as I am sure it has or will strike you, that when the need arises to deal forthrightly on your child's behalf, we are all essentially amateurs.

Eventually, I got the teacher's attention (by pulling strings, I am not especially proud to say) and my daughter received the help she needed. But if I had not known it before, I learned it then. Parents are all in the same boat, driven by the same impulses, beset by the same worries, frustrated by the same confusions, uplifted by the same thrills.

In fact, being a public school parent is like joining a large club. All members are equal. What we want for our children is roughly the same, regardless of what jobs we hold, where we stand on the social ladder, or how well or poorly we performed in our own school days.

And this belatedly dawned on me when my daughter desperately sought help for her math difficulties. On the occasion of that first rebuff from a world I thought I perfectly understood, I joined the club.

This book is my way of saying to you, welcome to the club!

And I say it with hearty enthusiasm. For I truly believe there may be no social affiliation in contemporary America that offers more, and *means* more, than being a public school parent.

For starters, you meet a lot of other parents experiencing highly charged ups and downs that overlap with your own. Some will be your friends, others will not. But with all of them you will have something in common.

You will share information and anecdotes and strategies with people who previously had been strangers but now appear more like colleagues. You will pitch in and help out alongside neighbors as well as new faces from the far side of town. You will find yourself delighted by amusing gossip and embroiled in heated discussions—discussions, I might add, with some very important ramifications for our national well-being.

If you want to stay on the sideline, you are free to make that choice. If you want to plunge in headfirst, you'll be in good company.

Parenting a public school child is a wonderful, exhilarating trip and I would not have missed it for the world. The experience can sometimes mark an almost surreal, even haunting return to your own school days. The rows of desks and chairs. The hallways bursting with life. The smudged chalkboards etched with words and calculations, crisp answers to vanished questions. So much of it still looks unchanged.

Here you are again! In the classroom. Chewing on your pencil. Eager, anxious, ready . . . sort of.

Yes, it's an amazing journey. But you are far more than a visitor or tourist. And, despite a lot of rhetoric being tossed around to this effect, you are far more than a mere consumer or customer. Your job is important, your influence potentially great. Is there a name for what you are?

There is. You are the New Public School Parent!

The goal of this book is to help you steer the best course for your child amidst the increasingly complex world of public schools. Many parents have experienced that anxious sinking feeling of being confronted with a pressing school dilemma only to discover you lack a basic understanding of what the issue involves, what solutions might be possible, and what your responsibilities and rights are. This book will, in effect, decode for you the shifting and often perplexing experience of public schools.

Schools, of course, do not set out to baffle parents. But for a variety of reasons, having largely to do with conflicting priorities and inefficient communication, schools remain for many parents a foreign, confounding place.

Similarly, the great flood of relevant and exciting information newly available about teaching methods, curriculum options, child psychology, and technology in the classroom—to list but a few—has not emerged expressly to bewilder parents. But bewilderment is what many of you, desperate to make sense of it, have come to feel.

This book aims also to be an empowerment tool, advocating in no uncertain terms that your child's schooling will be immeasurably enhanced by your ability to deftly navigate on his or her child's behalf. I'm tempted to recite the mountain of statistical evidence indicating that students perform far better when their parents are actively involved in their public school experience.

But you know that already.

This book sets out to inform you of how schools respond to certain situations, how teachers react to various problems, and ultimately what you can do to make sure that your child gets the best education possible.

The complicated psychodynamics between you and your child, while admittedly important, are not for the most part the subject of this book. I do not offer surefire, nine-step summaries of how you can motivate your children to do their homework, for example. (In my estimation, nobody can.)

My expertise lies directly in the area of schools and teachers, and my goal is to accurately convey to you all that I have learned from over 35 years in education about how schools work and how to make them work for you, the New Public School Parent.

In some of the real-life stories used to illustrate aspects of this book, the names of people have been changed, largely to protect the identity of the children involved.

1

The Child-Friendly School

When you walk through the corridors of your child's school, what sights do you see? Is the light bright enough? What sounds do you hear? Can you hear the happy chattering? Can you hear yourself think?

Try to sense the mood. Is it solemn? Festive? Chaotic? Disciplined?

A little of each? None of the above? Do you know which you'd like it to be?

Imagine yourself as a shorter person inhabiting these hallways. What would it be like? Would you feel intimidated or feel like you owned the place? Would you feel comfortable, detached, awed, involved? Look for the answers to those questions in the faces of the children passing by.

This is where your child spends her days. This is her true home away from home. This is where she learns—from teachers, from classmates, from peers, from carefully crafted lesson plans as well as surprise encounters that nobody can predict.

What's life like between these walls? It's important for you to know.

Over the past six years, I may have visited more public schools than anyone in the country. I have visited schools in the most densely populated streets of our largest cities. I have been in rural schools that students travel fifty miles to get to. I have visited schools in the leafy suburbs and on the asphalt fringes of industrial zones. Hundreds of them altogether.

After a while you develop an instinct, a sort of sixth sense about when a situation is right and when something's amiss.

I have learned to enter a public school with my antenna up,

1

with all my senses engaged. I observe the walls. The classrooms. The offices. The common areas, the cafeteria and library and playground. The swirl and flow of people. The *atmospherics*.

Let's take a tour. Schools are beehives of activity, not museum exhibits. There can be pockets of disarray. As we proceed, remember that what we seek to discover is the essence underlying the surface details.

The Hallways

You can learn a lot about your child's school by simply lingering a while in the hallways.

At a child-friendly school, children move about with ease and comfort and assuredness. And appropriate self-restraint. The child-friendly school allows freedom, but not at the expense of decorum.

Watch as students and staff pass by each other. Is there familiarity and trust between them? Are smiles exchanged, or is the mood one of guarded cohabitation? You'd like the children to feel like the place is theirs, so long as they abide by guidelines.

Discipline and order should be understated yet apparent. Let's face it, a building occupied by hundreds of rambunctious kids is bound to show volatility and outbursts of racket. But these should be the exception, not the rule. This means hallways should be generally subdued, if not always peaceful. Running and shoving, if they exist, should be short term and soon reined in.

What do you see on the walls? What type of student work is featured? You'd like to be met with a cornucopia of it, from artwork to graphic projects to poems and illustrated pieces of writing. I also like to see prints and reproductions of work by the masters. It never hurts to expose children to art at the highest level.

Displays of student art, by the way, ought not to be restricted solely to the most accomplished and talented (yes, all the school's children have their talents).

Check out the displays of class projects located outside the classrooms or in the vestibule. You can learn a lot this way, not just about the subject areas but about the students themselves.

What personal details come through? You should get a sense of children encouraged to be themselves, to *reveal* themselves, to respect themselves. There should be examples of personal essays and poems, artwork that expresses autobiographical details, celebrations of multiculturalism and other differences, slogans urging empathy and togetherness.

Do lobby displays attempt to correspond with seasonal or shared events—Thanksgiving, Martin Luther King, Jr., Day, an election, springtime?

The child-friendly school realizes that learning goes best when it's linked with the students' lives.

Classrooms

Notice the layout. There will always be desks or tables, and it's hard to avoid arranging these in rows. But what else is there?

Are pockets sectioned off for small group gatherings, for reading or artwork or experimentation? You'd like to see corners carved out for clusters of children to work together, and for children to go off by themselves.

How about the walls and bulletin boards? There should be lively, colorful supplements to ongoing class work, maps and posters and magazine cutouts illustrating matters under discussion. These need not be professionally produced and meticulously mounted. Teacher-made materials often appear in the classrooms of teachers who care.

Shelves should be busy. In the lower grades, they should be filled with beads and cloth and paper and paints; in the higher grades with age-appropriate manipulatives and learning resources: microscopes, geological specimens, scale-model pieces of machinery, palpable objects that can make learning less abstract.

Not all schools have ample resources, but simple materials used wisely are often preferable to the expensive store-bought kind.

What's your first impression of the teacher? Does he seem to praise and encourage the students? Does he move about, offering individual attention where needed? Does he show patience, enthusiasm?

Good teachers come in many, many shapes, ages, sizes, educational backgrounds, intellectual preferences, and personal styles. But they tend to have a few things in common: they're organized; they know their subject matter; they're confident in their abilities; and they care.

It may take more than a quick glance to scout for these qualities, but in the child-friendly classroom you'll find them.

The School Office

The central office where you find the principal, the secretary, and often the nurse is the command hub of the school.

It should be easy to locate. If at all possible, the office should be centrally located, open, and accessible. Upon entering the school, there should be a sign directing you there and notifying you that you're at the right spot.

School should be a welcoming, helpful, and totally open place. The office should give you and the students the feeling of a place where you can walk in unannounced and get your concerns swiftly attended to. The room should be inviting. The noise level should be conducive to serious business. This is a place where you'd like your child to be known by name, grade, and teacher. It is, after all, where you'll need to go when you or your child need to get things done.

If you're a visitor, some schools require you—for security reasons—to pick up a pass at the office. I've seen parents issued passes that read "team member" rather than "visitor." Certainly, that is the spirit in which you should be received.

In most public schools, there is a school **secretary** or **admin-**

istrative assistant who occupies a position of central importance far beyond what the title suggests. The school office is where you find this person.

It's a little secret of public schools that if you really need to know what's going on, if you really need to get something done—pronto!—the school secretary is probably who you want to see. This is the person who will get a message to your child or your child's teacher if needed. This is the person who will arrange a meeting for you with the principal. This is the person who will coordinate alternative transportation when a bus breaks down, and who will comfort your child if she misses the bus.

Stop by. Ask to speak with whoever is in charge of the central office. Introduce yourself. Have a question or two to ask. How are you received? Ask the secretary's name. This is a person you will quite probably have to rely on more than once.

Often the **principal**'s office adjoins the central office or is nearby.

The principal plays the role of ship captain, roaming the halls or sitting in on classes or greeting the morning buses. Her influence extends to virtually every aspect of the school, from curriculum to class assignments to policies on homework.

I've met enough principals over the years to know there is no reliable way to generalize about the type of person who makes a good one. Leadership ability is key, but that can take many forms. I've seen the job performed admirably by big personality extroverts as well as by quieter managers diligently doing good things.

The principal needs to be a problem-solver who can make tough decisions while retaining the respect of teachers and parents—two diverse constituencies that can be difficult to please.

The principal will be a reliable presence—sympathetic, competent, deft at balancing the myriad demands for individualized treatment with an enlightened overview of what works best for the whole.

Browse the **library** or **media center** at your child's school. It should be nicely lit and welcoming, with designated areas to sit and read or work quietly.

Note how the library and media center are used. Can students stroll in on their own or in clusters, without being accompanied by an adult? Do they go about their tasks with familiarity and comfort? Is there a librarian, media specialist, or volunteer to help out?

Is there a separate early reader section? What other resources are offered? Computers? Challenging and worthwhile software programs? Atlases and reference books?

A good school library/media center fills multiple needs—a place for advanced students to pursue independent work, a place for faltering readers to find suitable books, a calm and serious place for children to spend spare time.

The **cafeteria** and **playground** are arenas of considerable significance in the daily lives of students. When your child comes home at the end of the day, you are as likely—actually, more likely—to hear a story about the many interactions that occur at lunch or recess as you are to learn what new math concepts were conquered that day.

The cafeteria and playground are, however, places notoriously prone to mayhem. Few schools can claim to manage these chaotic environments with flawless efficiency. After all, lunch and recess provide much-needed opportunities for energetic children to loosen up and blow off steam.

It helps to have a fair number of adult monitors, and it helps if the room is not overly crowded.

Stick your head in. The cafeteria may not strike you as exactly the place you'd like to sit down and eat lunch. The playground may appear a bit wild and chaotic for your recreational tastes. But if the smiles on the children are genuine and the squeals are mostly of delight, if basic notions of safety and respect are reasonably maintained, that's mostly what counts.

Good **communication** with parents is essential. The school should try to make it easier for you to learn what your child is learning.

Many schools feature a regular newsletter to parents that, like a good community newspaper, reports on developments of general interest (new teachers, creation of a science club) and provides a calendar of upcoming events (school plays, workshops, school council meetings).

Principals sometimes sponsor early morning coffees for parents, either to address topics of concern or as an open-ended means of hearing what parents have on their mind.

One of the greatest challenges for a school is how to deal with unexpected "incidents," from fights to vandalism to natural catastrophes, which can generate a flood of rumors and confusion. Schools should have the capability of rapidly issuing bulletins to students and parents in order to clarify such situations.

Increasingly, schools have websites that can convey a range of information: a calendar of events, updates about school closings and other emergencies, as well as curriculum information and homework assignments in individual classrooms.

Through such devices, the child-friendly school makes a point of acknowledging that keeping parents informed is a key element of its mission.

Parental participation in the school should be encouraged.

Tutoring, monitoring, assisting in class or the library, chaperoning on field trips, and more ought to be welcomed.

Yes, there may be some successful public schools where an insular, controlling principal and a wary staff have fostered the habit of keeping parents at bay, places where you deliver your child first thing in the morning and nothing more is needed of you until taking your child back at day's end.

But the child-friendly school understands that you have a lot to offer, and is not shy about letting you know it. Recently, I've seen some schools that even set aside a separate room for parents to congregate and relax.

Information You Can't Get at a Glance but Might Be Able to Gather With a Few Quick Questions

- What is the school's average class size?
- Is there a limit to class size?
- What percentage of the faculty has been at the school more than ten years?
- What is the annual turnover among teachers?
- Are teachers certified to teach what they are assigned to teach?
- Are major repairs or renovations planned?
- What programs exist to meet the needs of individual students?
- Do teachers have a role in creating curriculum?
- Is there an active PTA or parents' group whom should you contact?

All this is public information. And all of this matters. You shouldn't have a problem getting the answers.

The Big Picture

I want to be clear about one aspect of this tour you've just taken. Schools that fall short in many superficial respects are perfectly capable of a superb performance where it unquestionably counts the most—educating children.

A school need not resemble some Disneyworld ideal and need not be uniformly populated by ever-smiling children and adults. Interior stairwells and halls don't have to unwaveringly employ uplifting pastels. The principal does not have to be as dynamic as Oprah Winfrey and not all teachers must prove as empathetic as Mister Rogers.

Schools in sorry need of repair often possess a spirit and vision that far outstrips any shortcomings in window dressing. Conversely, spanking new schools with gleaming windows and un-scuffed corridors can fail to do the job without a philosophy and commitment to being child-friendly.

I want to stress that these tips are not intended as a consumer report. Although my attention to the physical details of schools may sound like a tune-up for a shopping expedition, I completely reject the notion—popular in some circles—that public school parents are consumers.

No way! Your role is far more important than that of a mere consumer. If anything, your role is that of a partner—a full-fledged partner.

You want the best for your child, and you intend to be involved in making sure that happens. Let's go!

2

A Quality Teacher
for Your Child

What will my child's teacher be like? It's the question on the tip of every parent's tongue, the question which causes parents the most anxiety. Hey, I was an experienced teacher when my children first went off to school, and the matter caused me plenty of concern.

As well it should. Over the course of the school year, the teacher will become like a close relative taken under your roof, spending as much or more time with your child (at least K–5) as you do. The teacher will occupy a place of incredible importance in the life of your child. No aspect of schooling is more crucial. Your objective is clear: You want the best teacher you can get.

And yet you're beset with a feeling of semi-helplessness. There doesn't seem to be much you can actually do to ensure your child has a quality teacher, and it annoys you to leave a matter of such vital concern seemingly to chance. Yet that is exactly what the school's sometimes nebulous administrative processes seem to dictate.

I have been there, as a parent seeking ways to maneuver my daughters into what I felt were more favorable classrooms, and as a teacher hoping to avoid certain notoriously "difficult" students. As a practical matter, schools must strive for fairness and balance.

Thus, we have rules and procedures governing class assignments. Schools are increasingly reluctant, for a host of fairly reasonable reasons, to permit parents to select their child's teacher. This can leave you feeling vaguely screened off, as though you were a visitor to a military base and had only a limited security clearance. You're having difficulty gaining access to the places where you need to go.

You talk to other parents. You ask questions. You hear rumors. So-and-so got the teacher she wanted. How'd she do it?

You speak with teachers and the principal. It's a little weird because they seem to know more than they're allowed to tell. What's going on here? Why can't you get what you want?

In the course of this chapter, I will try to explain what is meant by a "quality teacher," what to look for in a teacher, and how schools struggle with this complex issue.

But I also want to broaden the discussion to encompass ways you can make the most of imperfect situations, and encourage your child to do likewise. Schools are human environments, subject to human influences, inhabited by accommodating people who strive to do well.

There is more to the issue of teacher quality than simply doing your utmost to maneuver the optimal class assignment, important as that may be. Regardless of your child's final placement, you actually have a greater degree of control than you might think over how the teacher performs and how your child reacts.

Can "Quality" Be Defined in a Teacher?

Yes, there is a large degree of subjectivity regarding teachers that your child does or does not like, and this can impact their effectiveness.

But the issue of "quality" begins with "qualified." This *can* be defined. Your child's teacher should:

- Be licensed to teach
- Be licensed to teach in the subject area to which he is assigned
- Participate in ongoing professional development that is aligned with student learning standards

- Be actively mentored (if they are in their first or second year of teaching) by a veteran teacher

Teaching is a profession. It is not, as California Governor Gray Davis once said, "a selfless act of patriotism, something young people will see as a cause that they will do for a limited period of time." It is not, as former Pennsylvania Governor Tom Ridge once proposed, a job that can be performed with just ten days of training.

Yes, most teachers choose their work because they love children and they love learning. But those attributes by themselves do not, and should not, qualify a person to teach your child.

Any parent who truly cares about her child's schooling must understand that the single greatest guarantee of a quality education is a trained, licensed, quality teacher who is a professional, who *sees* himself as a professional, and who *is treated* as a professional.

This may seem obvious but I need to state it anyway. If the professionalism of your child's teachers is undermined or compromised through watered-down standards or institutionalized disrespect, your child's schooling could, quite bluntly, be jeopardized.

Your school should have practices and policies in place that attract and encourage dedicated teachers. I have previously mentioned the notion of a child-friendly school. There is also, although not separately, such a thing as a teacher-friendly school.

Teacher-friendly schools are places where quality teachers are drawn to work. For quality teaching to flourish, there must be a supportive and hospitable environment. This includes:

- Manageable class sizes
- Flexibility to create and adapt curriculum
- Time during the normal workweek to meet with other faculty
- Time to pursue professional development opportunities
- Reasonable and competitive salaries

In addition, there are a number of traits and values repeatedly cited by parents, teachers, students, and administrators as key to a quality teacher:

- Knows the subject he or she is teaching
- Cares about the students
- Makes an effort to know each child's unique qualities and interests
- Sets high achievement goals, and works with all students to get there
- Maintains order and discipline without being oppressive
- Possesses good diagnostic skills
- Emphasizes self-assessment, so students don't just rely on grades to know how they're doing
- Teaches "fix-up" strategies to help students correct their mistakes
- Communicates regularly with parents, and alerts them promptly if there is cause for concern
- Treats all students fairly
- Makes learning fun and stimulating
- Recognizes when something is not going well with a student, and takes action
- Gives praise and encouragement

Think about this list. Imagine how difficult it would be to embody those qualities seven-plus hours a day, 180 days per year, under conditions that are, to put it mildly, unpredictable.

Teachers who manage to pull it off and finish each day with a buoyant smile are the ones you most want for your children. But not all teachers, not even good ones, can consistently measure up when they lack a supportive environment. It can be difficult for adults with other types of jobs to fully understand the unique pressures a teacher faces.

The essence of teaching has to be giving your all to every child. Now that doesn't mean you can do it every day. Nobody can be "up" all the time. As with parenting, you're going to have some bad days. When I had those kind of days, I learned to let my students know. "Today's not a good day for me," I might tell them. "Try to bear with me."

But a teacher has to be ready to bounce back. Pronto. There's a moral component to teaching; getting by is not good enough.

Evaluating the Teacher

From the start of the school year you will be engaged in evaluating your child's teacher, in ways that are either active or passive, low key or intense, overt or subconscious. Information about the quality of the teacher comes to you in four basic ways:

- Your child's impressions
- Conversations with other parents
- Visits to the classroom
- Interactions with the teacher

In my experience, teacher quality is complex and often subjective. Any parent should be cautious about reaching a firm conclusion in so crucial a matter without considering input from most of the above sources.

Even the best teachers can have a style or personality that rubs a child or parent the wrong way. A good teacher may have locked horns with influential parents, leading to a stream of suspicious rumors. A superior student may have transferred out of a well-respected teacher's class, for reasons that were not clear.

I know of one very talented elementary school teacher, formerly the "Teacher of the Year" in his state, who had several children eager to leave the class. "Quality" was, in this instance, not the problem. The teacher had unique, iconoclastic, decidedly nontraditional methods. For these students, it was simply a wrong fit.

Always keep that in mind.

For example, take what is probably the most common complaint: The teacher is "boring." You hear this complaint frequently from children. But what does it actually mean? Does it speak to "quality"?

"Boring," of course, can mean that a teacher is unengaged, uninspired, and uninspiring—all characteristics which would indeed constitute a highly flawed teacher.

But in evaluating this complaint, parents need to consider the source.

"Boring" may also indicate a teacher who emphasizes stern work habits, repetitive drills, and strict classroom discipline. Such a teacher may not be ideal. Such a teacher might lack imagination and creativity. But there is no reason to assume this is an incompetent teacher.

Here are some questions to help place the "boring" complaint in perspective:

- Is your child making strides in learning, both information and skills?
- Is the teacher knowledgeable about the subjects being taught?
- Does the teacher care about the children in the class?
- Does the class provide extra features—research projects, field trips—that can be stimulating?

I point these out not to exonerate boring teachers, but to encourage parents to face certain practical realities. Namely, there are times when your child is best served by accepting that this is the teacher with whom she will be spending the year. Especially when the problem at hand can be—if not solved—at least partially overcome.

In visiting the classroom, you should keep an eye out for:

- Children moving about and working happily
- What children are doing to stay occupied when the teacher is working with certain students
- Whether the teacher pays attention to many students or just a few
- Whether children appear comfortable and appreciated, or insecure
- Walls decorated with projects and student artwork

- Whether lessons are clearly explained
- Who is doing most of the talking
- Signs, such as wall displays, of rewards and recognition to motivate students
- Routine lessons and activities that appear rote and predictable to the kids
- Whether the teacher is organized and seems to enjoy his work

Seeking Input from Other Parents

Let's face it. You hear things. A primary way parents learn anything about teachers is through word-of-mouth.

You should probably speak to several sources before drawing any conclusion about a teacher based on input from other parents—especially if there is a problem or complaint. There are just too many variables in the interactions between a teacher and students to comfortably allow a blanket generalization based on one family's experience.

Points to consider in speaking with other parents:

- Do they hear comments from their children similar to what you have heard?
- Does their experience differ widely from yours?
- Have they spoken with the teacher about their concern, and was any action taken?
- Have they approached the principal regarding this teacher, and what was the result?

As a former teacher, I am certainly not trying to persuade you to scrutinize every move the teacher makes. On the contrary, I believe that much of the good work that teachers perform takes place below the radar screen of parents, who are not in the classroom every day. Rather, my point is that if you are going to engage in evaluating the teacher—and it's hard not to—then make sure you seek a broad view from multiple perspectives.

And remember, as my colleague David Sheridan remarked, schools are run by muggles, not gods.

What Are Some Characteristics of a "Bad" Teacher?

The following qualities are unacceptable in a teacher:

- Does not know the subject area
- Loses patience quickly and often
- Cannot maintain order or does so only through yelling and threats
- Plays favorites and belittles lesser students
- Lacks enthusiasm
- Possesses rigid, narrow view of learning
- Is overwhelmed by the demands for multitasking
- Is erratic and inattentive with homework assignments
- Lacks a varied and differentiated approach to students
- Communicates ineffectively with parents

Also, schools desperate to fill vacancies are increasingly reaching out to underqualified individuals. Parents should be concerned if their school accepts as "qualified" teachers who lack credentials or formal training.

. . . .

Cupertino, CA: "The Rich Teachers Are Coming!"

"The rich teachers are coming!" So declared a Sedgwick Elementary School student, explaining why he did not want to be pulled out of class for his regular speech resource session.

What the boy meant to say was that the "enrichment" teachers were coming, as they do at Sedgwick every Wednesday. These visits, popular with students and teachers alike for reasons I'll soon mention, have become like field trips without leaving the campus.

But the point of these sessions is to provide a break for teachers, not students. The purpose of the enrichment program is to offer classroom teachers an opportunity to observe the class of another teacher, and thereby learn from his or her techniques.

As first-grade teacher Amy Hansen, one of the founders of the program, explains, "There's never enough time for professional development. That's always the complaint that teachers have. With this program, we're trying to address that."

The "rich teachers" who make the program possible are, in fact, Sedgwick Elementary parents. Each year, several parents assume the role of designated substitutes on Wednesday mornings, freeing classroom teachers to periodically observe a fellow teacher and afterward confer with grade-level colleagues about what they have learned.

It sounds simple, but such opportunities, so instrumental to professional growth and improvement, are hard to come by in the careers of most teachers.

Here's how it worked one Wednesday morning last November. Shortly before the start of school, the enrichment parents gathered in the faculty room to review their schedule and take one last deep breath before plunging into the day's assignment, the always-daunting sixth grade. (Middle school starts in grade seven in the district.)

Kate Whittley had come prepared. A former teacher, Kate is a mother of two boys at Sedgwick. She understands the need in her substitute stint to strike a delicate balance between learning and entertainment. Her lesson, which she would perform before each of the school's three sixth-grade classrooms (alternating rooms with two other parents who would prepare their own lessons), will focus on aviation and invention.

Kate entered the classroom. Melissa Riley, the regular teacher, cautioned the students to show respect and then walked down the hallway to a third-grade class to learn more about conducting class meetings.

Now I bet that class meetings are a part of teaching you've not given much thought to. As it turns out, neither have most schools of education and teacher preparation programs. Class meetings are what you'd guess: formal gatherings for the express purpose of collectively talking through issues or problems that merit the attention of the entire group. If properly conducted, class meetings can help in building class unity and spirit, and improving the climate for learning.

With this and other facets of classroom management, teachers usually are hungry to know the answer to a common yet elusive question: Is what I'm doing okay? Am I doing this right?

With this program, Sedgwick has devised an excellent way for teachers to know the answers to these questions: Observe what their fellow teachers do.

In Melissa Riley's sixth-grade classroom, parent-substitute Kate Whittley began her lesson by explaining that invention comes in many forms, that it need not require sophisticated scientific knowledge. To illustrate, she passed out a sheet of paper detailing the story of Walt Morrison, alleged creator of the frisbee.

Meanwhile, along another corridor, Melissa Riley and two more sixth-grade teachers took seats in the back of the room to observe a veteran third-grade teacher, Erin Sharps, conducting a class meeting. There are two schools of thought (at least) about class meetings: Schedule them at regular, predictable intervals, or call them as the need arises. Each method has its merits, and the sixth-grade teachers at Sedgwick have briefly discussed these before entering the room.

Erin's class meeting was of the regularly scheduled type. She began by asking her students to close their eyes and try to visualize an ideal class situation: how the day begins, the unfolding of their mini-lessons, recess on the playground, the reading workshop, etc.

Next, the teacher asked the children to offer up a list of class behavior improvements they'd like to see in order to make that ideal day more possible. Hands shot up; Erin jotted the suggestions onto the board for all to see: take turns in science; don't make fun of others; don't give answers away in math; don't be silly at music; use kind voices.

Meanwhile, Kate Whittley had handed out to the sixth graders several fun projects: Lego model airplane kits, diagrams for the construction of paper airplanes, and—the grand finale—a makeshift hot air balloon that the students would attempt to launch in the playground adjoining the school. The sixth graders leapt to their tasks.

Back in the third-grade class, the steps of the class meeting proceeded. Erin asked the children to select an item listed on the board which they believed to be especially important, and to explain how the class could benefit with the correction of this problem. Speaking up in front of their classmates was a challenge for many of the children. ("It's a problem getting the ones who don't talk to talk," Melissa noted during the post-observation discussion.)

Back in Melissa's sixth-grade classroom, the Lego airplane models were mostly assembled. Some students were working on paper airplanes, nearly gleeful at gaining permission to launch these normally prohibited items. "Wait until we're outside," Kate warned one eager boy.

On the patio by the exit door, other students applied hair dryers (brought by Kate) to the underside of the four-foot-tall hot air balloon that Kate had assembled from specialized paper at home.

Enrichment parents, it should be noted, are paid modestly for their efforts—$17 per hour covers classroom time but not preparation time, which Kate estimates at several hours or more per week. According to Sedgwick principal, Lynn Shimata, by California law, adults can only be left solely in charge of a classroom if they are a paid independent contractor.

At the conclusion of the class meeting (which did not formally conclude since time ran out before the final stage where students offer ways to implement the suggested improvements), Erin and the sixth-grade teachers retreated to the faculty room for a round-table talk. Like connoisseurs of an art form, the teachers focused on nuances of what took place that a lay person might not have detected.

For example, Erin's use of a gently impartial tone of voice in recording the list of correctable behaviors was commended. "We know you can be tough," Melissa commented. Teachers questioned Erin about the use of visualization at the start of the meeting, noting that such a technique probably would not work with sixth graders. The selection of topics for class meetings was discussed. Melissa floated the idea of using a suggestion box to encourage anonymous feedback from students who might not want to have their classmates identify them with a particular concern.

"The key," Erin reminded the teachers, "is to have the kids get connected to each other, to build unity."

Unity seemed to be mounting with the balloon launch outside the sixth-grade classroom. Two students standing on chairs with hair driers had gotten the balloon to inflate. The moment had arrived. Driers were switched off. The entire class gathered to watch.

Kate again hurriedly explained the principles of hot air rising in relation to the surrounding cold. But the morning sun had risen with precarious warmth across the patio. "This might not work," she warned.

The students holding the balloon stepped back to let her fly. For an instant, the balloon hesitated as if considering liftoff, then promptly shriveled.

"So much for this experiment." commented Kate. But she said it with a satisfied smile. For the experiment that had brought her into the class was working exactly as planned.

....

Getting the Most out of Your Child's Teacher

For most students in most schools, the classroom teacher will be a man or woman with many talents, and perhaps some flaws. The teacher may well be imperfect. That happens. Teachers are only human, after all.

In such situations, I feel it is important for parents to focus less on the teacher's shortcomings (not rigorous about math, not very exciting, etc.) and emphasize what it is that the teacher does well. Most teachers have a lot to offer, and it is important for you to orient your child to a positive and productive attitude.

I am not talking about covering up or burying your head in the sand. But I am speaking of reviving an oft-overlooked feature of parenting a public school child: making the best of the situation.

There are countless examples of parents' initial disappointment with a teacher transforming over the course of a school year into sheer delight as underappreciated qualities (a keen knowledge of nature, a nuanced sense of the child's special interests) rise to the forefront.

Ultimately, learning how to work with the teacher is an essential part of your child's education. In fact, the only teacher I would be tempted to write off as "impossible" would be one who is too inflexible or too unconcerned to want to discuss a better way.

While I completely empathize with your urge to seek the best possible classroom for your child, I feel there are parents who sometimes go too far in seeking to maneuver out of classroom situations that are inherently positive but contain some rough edges. Adaptation and dealing with minor dissatisfactions are as much a part of school culture as they are the general culture, and are an integral part of your child's growth and education.

It is important to remember that even a teacher who may not be to your child's liking remains, nonetheless, a teacher from whom your child stands to learn quite a lot. Without stretching too far for the silver lining, it is my belief that a less skilled or less experienced teacher can offer a hidden chance for you—and your child—to learn the essential art of making the most from imperfect situations.

Taking this path is often much easier and far less disruptive than switching teachers.

What Can Be Done About a Bad Teacher?

Let's face it. Your child may, regrettably, wind up at some point with a teacher who is either incompetent or temperamentally unsuited for the job. It is an extremely distressing situation.

I could explain to you the encouraging developments that are taking place to identify and find ways to remove poor teachers (as president of the nation's largest teachers union, I broke new ground by taking on this issue). But I know that at the time your child is suffering, languishing, or being underserved, the big picture is not what concerns you. You want a change, and you want it soon.

If you have concluded unequivocally that your child has such a teacher, you have only a few options:

First, you need to take the matter up directly with the teacher. You need to do this both as a matter of protocol (at all subsequent stages, you will be asked by the principal or other school staff: Have you addressed this with the teacher?) and for the satisfaction of doing your best to be fair. This discussion can be especially hard if you suspect that the teacher is simply not up to the job.

If talking directly to the teacher proves ineffective, and if your child is not learning and her attitude toward school is disintegrating, you have no choice but to take the next step: Contact the principal.

Complaints about teachers are awkward for school administrators, but most are veterans at handling them. The principal will probably want to arrange a meeting between you and the teacher. The purpose of this will be to explore ways the teacher can better accommodate your child.

You may be skeptical that the teacher can ever adequately do the job. Still, the principal may well be obligated to pursue this course, and you will need to go along with it.

If the problem is academic (i.e. your child is not being adequately taught or serious learning needs are going unattended) the principal may attempt to fashion supplemental activities or a team arrangement with another teacher to help out.

If the problem is a bad personal dynamic between the teacher and your child, the principal may explore mediation-type methods for cultivating a better relationship.

If no solution emerges or if attempted solutions fail to improve your child's situation, switching teachers is the logical option. Keep in mind that schools are reluctant to reach this conclusion, for reasons you can well imagine. It sends a questionable message to parents whose children remain in the same classroom, and can be perceived by staff members as a failure of support.

"Finessing" the decision to switch is thus something to which all parties—the principal, the teacher, and you—will need to pay careful attention.

Getting the Teacher You Want for Your Child

"Shopping for teachers," as the practice is known, is both widespread among public school parents and frequently met with frustration. Each school has its own way of handling class assignments, and you will probably have to spend some time speaking with other parents to figure out how the game works, if it works at all.

The single across-the-board truism is that if you have a clear idea of which teacher you want for your child, your best chance for succeeding is before the placements have been formally announced.

Some schools permit you to overtly request a teacher for the next year, and are only compelled to make tough decisions when a certain classroom is oversubscribed. The process of requesting is fairly straightforward.

You should do your research regarding the strengths and weaknesses of the optional teachers. And, of course, you should know what type of teacher works best for your child—which may not be the same as what type of teacher your child most enjoys.

Increasingly, however, many principals prefer to work out next year's class configurations in private conference with teachers and perhaps the guidance counselor. They do it this way to avoid an onslaught of high pressure and potentially disruptive lobbying by parents.

Even then, it's possible to make your request known to those in charge. One Jackson, Mississippi, mother of two public school children reported this casual interchange with the assistant principal on bumping into him one morning.

> *Mother:* "I know I'm not supposed to, but I want to request a teacher for next year."
>
> *Asst. Principal:* rolls his eyes, but says nothing.
>
> *Mother:* "For third grade, I'd really like to see my son get __."
>
> *Asst. Principal:* "You know I can't promise you anything."

Her son was assigned the requested teacher.

When a school does not permit you to directly request next year's teacher, you can indirectly make a case for a certain teacher. In making assignments, administrators do strive to find the optimal learning situation for each student if there is evidence that one classroom might be more conducive than another.

One way to accomplish this is by citing to the principal or school psychologist (preferably with documentation) how your child's learning style would benefit from being matched with a teacher of corresponding strengths.

Principals who are usually quite aware of the capabilities of their faculty are nonetheless reluctant to openly acknowledge shortcomings; your appeal should accentuate the positive: how your child will be served by a certain teacher's virtues.

In making class placements, principals openly consider a host of issues, both social and academic, which enable them to find the best fit for each child while establishing balanced classes. It is acceptable and appropriate for you to bring relevant features about your child to the attention of the principal. I suggest setting up a meeting during the spring or summer, before next year's class placements are made. (If a meeting is not possible, you can write a letter conveying the same information.)

This meeting with the principal is your chance to underscore the characteristics you believe should impact class placement. Keep in mind that you are doing this with an eye toward which teacher represents the most promising fit . Thus, for example, it can be useful for you to point out your child's:

- Preference for a warm and supportive teacher
- Need for a teacher strong in reading difficulties
- Need for a very orderly classroom
- Preference for arts-oriented instruction

"My daughter is shy and can slip through the cracks," you might say, angling for the extrovert teacher known to emphasize teamwork among students.

"My son does best in an environment with traditional instruction and no fooling around," you might state, hoping for the disciplinarian who did wonders for your older boy.

Maybe the principal will ask you questions. Chances are she will have reviewed your child's file, which may or may not contain verification of these contentions. Do not expect the principal to reveal very much to you in these meetings. It's possible that you can make an airtight case, and the principal will have no choice but to agree.

It's more likely, however, that you'll have to be satisfied with knowing you've inserted an additional factor into the class assignment deliberations: all things equal, why not place your child where you think is best?

Note of caution: Teacher assignment is far from an exact science. Too many parents, understandably avid to do right by their children, approach this as though it were a wholly methodical process. Let me cite some of the reasons why it is not:

- Children can change from year to year
- Teachers can change
- What was good for one sibling in a family might not be good for another

I mention this because I fear that many parents set themselves up for frustration by falsely assuming that the skills they rely on in their professional lives—gathering facts, weighing information, sizing up situations and coming to a determination—will guide them just as successfully when it comes to decisions about their child's schooling.

If only it were so!

Substitute Teachers

Schools have varying guidelines for hiring substitute teachers. As with the general teacher population, schools prefer substitutes to be licensed but in an emergency, which is often the case, they make accommodations.

Substitutes are potentially an important part of your child's school experience, especially if your child's regular teacher is ever absent for more than a week straight.

The following are questions you might ask of the principal if your child's classroom requires a substitute teacher on a recurring basis.

- Is the substitute licensed, and licensed specifically in the area where he is assigned?
- Is the substitute known to be competent?
- Has the substitute been briefed about the culture of the school, and its mission?
- Is the substitute regularly mentored by a teacher of the same grade level who has been trained to do mentoring?
- Has the substitute been in communication with the regular teacher and received all relevant documents from that teacher?
- Has the substitute been briefed by the regular teacher concerning what lessons to review, and which lessons are most successful?
- Has the substitute been warned not to introduce new material and lessons?

Relevant Facts

- The quality which parents say they most want from their child's teacher is "caring"
- 30–40 percent of teachers are teaching out of the field where they are trained
- Only one in five new teachers is adequately mentored
- 13–15 percent of teachers are not licensed
- Only the states of Texas and Georgia have laws requiring schools to notify parents if the teacher is not licensed

What Measures Should a School Have in Place to Boost Teacher Quality?

When I first appeared before the National Press Club after taking over as NEA president, I was asked if the problem was not so much with bad teachers but with mediocre ones. "Mediocrity is no longer acceptable in education," the questioner contended, "given how quickly students need to learn to make themselves competitive."

My answer to that was—and is—that school systems have a responsibility to help teachers improve.

It amazes me that when we talk about teachers we seem to forget how the private sector and the world of business handle similar concerns. In those arenas, when new knowledge is disseminated, when new techniques are developed, the company makes certain that its employees are brought up to speed and trained to function in this evolving environment.

Does your school take responsibility for providing its teachers with adequate professional development?

When new technologies are brought into the classroom, are the teachers trained in how to utilize it?

As new teaching strategies are developed, are the teachers introduced to them?

Does the school provide regular opportunities for teachers to share information, and learn from each other?

When there are shifts in curriculum, what help do teachers receive in adjusting?

Does any of this matter? How could it not?

The Big Picture

I learned early on as a middle-school teacher that there is a harsh gap between theories for how to manage educational systems and the urgent demands of the young people who are being impacted every single day.

Parents sending their sons and daughters off to their first day of kindergarten confront a reality that every educator and policy maker should always keep in mind: The next thirteen years will be the most precious in that child's life. Every decision that gets made is, in some basic way, vital.

And that applies to teacher quality.

Study after study has shown that the single greatest determinant in the success of a child's schooling is the quality of the classroom teacher. As the National Commission on Teaching and America's Future put it, "No other intervention can make the difference that a knowledgeable, skillful teacher can make in the learning process. Students learn more when their teacher knows more."

Now that is fairly straightforward.

I have mentioned this frequently in my various meetings and school facility tours with political and business leaders concerned about the fate of our schools. Armed as many of these leaders are with an energetic, can-do self-assurance, they will often turn to me and say, "So? Why don't schools just go out and hire top-quality teachers?"

At such moments, I don't know whether to laugh or cry.

So many people who have no trouble understanding the critical importance of quality teachers have, oddly enough, a great deal of trouble in understanding the simple and concrete steps that should be taken to improve the situation.

There is no mystery in the professional world about how to maximize the quality of personnel: decent pay and working conditions, adequate training and support services.

So why the seeming bafflement in the field of education? It amazes me that people would opt to leave to the whimsy of chance a situation (quality teaching for your child) that could be vastly improved by a sensible commitment to teacher recruitment and retention. I am sure of one thing: The way to improve the chance of your child being assigned a quality teacher *is not* to hope and pray for that brilliant and energetic soul (although plenty of them exist in the teacher ranks) who couldn't care less about salary.

The news is full of stories about the growing teacher shortage. To my mind, there is not so much a teacher shortage as there is a respect shortage, a salary shortage, an acute shortage of the most basic care and feeding of teachers in their professional lives.

What does it say about our priorities when we *say* we want the best and brightest to enter teaching, and yet we pay new teachers as little as $20,000 in some states? (Nationally, the average public-school teacher salary for grades K–12 is approximately $40,600.)

Does upgrading the wages and improving the working conditions guarantee a first-rate teacher? Of course not. Teaching, as I know quite well, is not like other professions. But to speak of teacher quality—something we should and *must* speak of—without addressing core realities of how to attract, train, cultivate, and encourage teachers is simply dishonest.

When I think about this critical issue—and I think it about it a lot—I am struck by a missing element in the discussion. And that is the voice of the community, of parents and civic leaders. Individuals have their say as the occasion arises, and that is as it should be.

But can you imagine the community outcry if there was a shortage of quality medical care? Or a shortage of any other professional service that was deemed important?

There would be public meetings to mobilize opinion. There would be strategy sessions to formulate action plans. Commentators and opinion makers would leap to the cause. Legislators would be lobbied, and soon would put forth urgent proposals. Governors would intervene. There would be an overarching sense that we are all in this together. All for one and one for all.

But when it comes to quality teaching, a feature of civic life that may be second in importance—if that—only to medical care in the minds of many families, there is an almost total void.

Teacher quality is an issue that cries out for more. It deserves to be explored by ad hoc meetings of concerned citizens, by special sessions of the city council, by round table gatherings of business chieftains. It's up to you and fellow members of this new generation of public school parents to make sure this happens.

3

When Your Child Is Falling Behind

Why does your child struggle where other kids seemingly learn so easily? Why can't he grasp lessons that ought to be almost second nature? Is it possible that he simply lacks some basic tool? What exactly is the problem?

Perhaps there have been warning signs, a slowness to read, a clumsiness with elementary math, or a general avoidance of learning challenges. You know he's bright enough. It's just that . . . it's just that he's doing so poorly.

Your heart may sink when it seems your child is falling seriously behind in school. It's not the end of the world, but it can sure feel like it. Your child may grow ornery and despondent. Every school day presents steeper new challenges—as if the old ones weren't already more than enough. You hope the cause is something, like poor study habits or a bad attitude, that can be easily identified and swiftly set straight.

But it's hard not to worry that more serious issues might lurk beneath.

I have experienced this predicament as a teacher and as a parent, and I know how intensely upsetting it can be. Don't panic. I can't assure you that everything will work out perfectly, but I can assure you that schools are equipped to handle this. Your school has been here before. Helping a struggling child is, in fact, the very stuff of what a public school should be about. In my experience, helping a floundering student is one of the most gratifying challenges in the field of education, and most teachers feel the same way.

Falling behind is a serious predicament. Your child's progress through the grades can be like a moving train. It is hard to catch up if you lag back too far.

At school, classes move at a (roughly) steady pace, building from lesson to lesson toward predetermined curriculum objectives. Teachers, the engineers of these trains, cannot afford many unscheduled delays if they intend to fulfill their obligation to arrive at the station on time (i.e. with the designated curriculum covered by year's end).

This need to keep the academic agenda moving forward at a calculated speed necessarily creates problems, most obviously for students who either learn at a slower rate or are prone to stumble in particular subject areas.

A child falling behind in class may indeed become like the train passenger left at the platform. The train moves steadily onward. Keeping up becomes increasingly difficult. For a while, it can seem like an accomplishment if you simply fall no further behind.

But unlike the passenger, the struggling student cannot always scramble to his feet and start racing forward. Instead, he is susceptible to syndromes and problems (estrangement from peers, plunging self-esteem) that can make it even more difficult to catch up.

As there are gifted learners, for whom the basic methods of schoolwork come with natural ease, so too are there children for whom academic learning is destined to be a struggle nearly every step of the way.

It's a situation that merits prompt attention and thoughtful intervention. The sooner, the better. Teachers know this and so should you.

How Do I Tell if the Situation Is Serious?

I am a big believer in parents going with their gut instincts. Nowhere is that more important than when it comes to whether or not your child is in serious academic trouble.

As with so many facets of school life, there are children whose difficulties are obvious and inarguable, and there are children whose problems are quite subtle and virtually undetectable. One of the most vexing dilemmas you can face as a parent is determining when, or if, your child is in academic trouble.

Parents I've known in this situation report a bewildering swirl of intense emotions that make it harder, not easier, to act wisely. The precipitous ups and downs of trying to learn what troubles your child amount to a staggering roller coaster ride that leaves few unscathed. You feel guilty (at having not noticed it sooner), frustrated (at the amount of work that lies ahead), and scared (that the solutions will not come easily). Most of all, you fear for your child's future.

Along the way, there are a host of hidden trap doors. You may find yourself elated at learning "nothing" is wrong, even when all your instincts tell you that something *is* wrong. You may find yourself nearly bereft at the first indication of a learning disability, when in fact it is precisely that discovery that will enable your child to get back on track.

Adding to the confusion is the fact that many of the standard indicators of falling behind are reasonably common to many children. Such as:

- Poor grades
- Failure to turn in homework
- Lackluster attitude toward school
- Sinking self-esteem

Whereas many children display these qualities at one time or another, there is a difference between a student who is merely having temporary difficulties and one who is on the brink of seriously dropping far behind the class.

How do you tell one from the other?

As educational consultant Lawrence Greene writes in *Finding Help When Your Child Is Struggling In School*, "The red flags signaling problems in scholastic performance, attitude, and/or behavior can be difficult to differentiate, so you must be prepared to do some sleuthing."

In my opinion, you have serious cause for concern if you detect that your child:

- Works reasonably hard yet is very frustrated at lack of results
- Shows academic achievement significantly behind the majority of classmates
- Expresses intense dislike of school
- Takes an excessive amount of time to complete homework
- Is markedly confused about grade-level subject areas
- Displays a short and erratic attention span
- Has poor reading fluency
- Does not study or seem to understand how to effectively study
- Is suffering low self-esteem related to school work
- Has not been helped by prior efforts to improve her schoolwork

Also, as Barbara Kapinus, a senior policy analyst at the NEA and a veteran reading specialist, points out, "It's important to find out if a child is not doing work because he can't or because he won't. Some times *can't* looks a lot like *won't.*

> *WARNING: Beware of being told that laziness is the major source of your child's troubles. This is a standard analysis some schools make of underachievers, and sometimes it is true. But laziness or a seeming lack of concern about bad performance often masks deeper, more complicated problems.*

How to Detect When Your Child Is Falling Behind

Identification that your child is in trouble or floundering generally is made in one of two ways: by an astute and trained teacher; by you or people close to your child.

A. Identification by the Teacher.

Ideally, your child's difficulties will be noticed and diagnosed by the classroom teacher. A savvy teacher knows what to look for, and knows that intervention is called for long before a failing or unsatisfactory grade is entered onto the report card.

The teacher is your early warning system. Good teachers are skilled observers of children. Moreover, a savvy teacher will be aware of grade-appropriate indicators that something is more than casually wrong.

The ability to diagnose students who are struggling is one of the truly cherished talents of the teaching profession. It is also a skill that can and should be taught, for its importance is fundamental. Astute teachers are continually on the lookout for basic sources of learning problems. These include:

- *Perception.* Does the student see and hear clearly and correctly?
- *Attention.* Does the student focus properly and consistently when it is important to do so?
- *Speech and motor skills.* Is the student in command of the mechanics of speaking and writing?
- *Mental health.* Is the student generally in a positive frame of mind?
- *Executive functions.* Does the student process information efficiently and methodically?

To this list, Dr. Ann Kaganoff, former president of the Association of Educational Therapists, adds another:

- *Instructional history.* Has the student done reasonably well and been decently taught in prior years?

B. Identification by You

You may lack a trained eye for discerning educational shortcomings. You may not be in a position to ascertain what is substandard or below average when it comes to grade-level achievement. But you do know your child. You know the body language and vocal tones that involuntarily reveal the truths which verbal statements sometimes try to hide.

It is not easy to step back and render an objective evaluation of your child. In fact, most parents are susceptible to a host of hidden urges to do exactly the opposite.

It can be profoundly sad to recognize that your child is floundering, particularly if there is a suspicion that the underlying causes might not be simple to solve.

But don't let your emotions interfere with your mission. You have a job to do, and it could be one of the most important ones you perform on your child's behalf. The list (above) that teachers heed is a fair guideline of things to watch for. In addition, at home you will want to take note if your child seems consistently lost and frustrated on homework, has intensely negative feelings about school, acts out or causes trouble to avoid schoolwork, and does not respond to the help that is being offered.

If you suspect your child is falling behind, don't hesitate to call for a conference with the teacher.

Similarly, the teacher should communicate to you any worrisome observations she might have. This should be done with as much specificity as possible. It is not enough for you to be told that your child is "having trouble" or "seems lost." You should be told precisely what has been observed, why it causes concern, and what the teacher's past experience has been with this type of situation.

You will want the teacher to offer some informed conjecture concerning the source of your child's problem, and what the school plans to do about it.

What Can the School Do?

Determining the cause of the problem will be your next important step. Basically, you will be looking to discover whether the difficulty is circumstantial (poor basics, under-motivation, class dynamics), which is to say problems that are correctable within the classroom framework, or due to learning difficulties.

As you begin to sort through this, you will want to find out:

- How far behind the class your child is
- If your child has been behind since the start of the class, or if it is a recent development
- What the teacher thinks the cause might be
- What are some strategies for closing the gap
- If this can be accomplished within the normal class time and structure
- How hard it will be for your child to catch up
- If a learning disability might be holding your child back

Your mind will be fraught with concerns. Is your child going to have to work harder than others? Or worse, will keeping up be hard even with extra effort?

Either way, you will need to be ready to act.

What Is the Child Study Team, and What Is Its Function?

A child study team (which can also be referred to as the student study team, pre-referral team, early intervention team, or student assistance team) is convened at the request of the classroom teacher who believes a student needs extra attention and can benefit from multiple perspectives. In effect, the gesture is the teacher's way of reaching out for additional advice and perspective.

Though not all schools choose to employ the study team method, its component parts (see below) are usually featured in how a school deals with a struggling student.

Typically, this team consists of the school psychologist, guidance counselor, resource specialist, other teachers, and anyone else who can provide information about the student. The classroom teacher is of course part of this team, and is the key figure.

Any decision that gets made will need to be approved and implemented by the teacher.

The purpose of this formal gathering is to attempt a more extensive evaluation of the student. This will include in-class observations, a review of the student's portfolio and standardized test scores, plus interviews with the teacher and other faculty familiar with the student's work.

Parents should be notified by the school when a study team is being convened for their child. Parents do not have the option of saying "no" to the process, however. They can, in some situations, attend the team meeting and have input into the process.

Veteran teachers with a large repertoire of strategies (having worked through similar situations in the past) may be less inclined to call on the child study team than newer teachers might be.

What Will the Child Study Team Do?

Basically, there are two stages to the team's effort: observation and data collection; intervention and documentation.

In the first stage, *observation and data collection,* the team will be extensively briefed by the classroom teacher and will be given access to relevant tests and schoolwork by the student.

A member may make visits to the class to observe habits of the student's which relate to the area of concern. Does the child fidget and frequently get out of her seat? Does she speak out of turn? Is she sullen and remote? Does she have difficulty with transitions? Does she need to have instructions repeated? The team observer will know what kinds of behavior could be related to the problem.

This process takes time. According to Patti Ralabate, chair of the child study team for Hayestown Avenue School, an elementary school in Danbury, Connecticut, "A good child study team will move slowly, and this can be frustrating to a parent."

How long should it take? One to two weeks ought to be enough time to make sufficient observations and gather other types of information from previous teachers, resource specialists, and possibly parents or guardians. Generally speaking, intervention should begin within a few weeks of the time the team first meets.

(Note: If the team determines that there is evidence of the child having a learning disability, the child will likely be referred to the special education multidisciplinary team, or MDT.)

The second stage is *intervention and documentation*. This is where the teacher puts into practice the various strategies the team has devised.

The range of possible measures is vast, depending on the diagnosis and the school's resources. They might include:

- Supplemental learning materials, printed as well as manipulatives (tactile, tangible, hand-held aids to learning)
- Modified work loads
- Providing a written (not just verbal) guideline to assignments
- Progress reports at frequent intervals
- Seating arrangement and group organization
- Allowing use of a calculator
- Allowing use of a computer if handwriting is an issue
- Instruction in study methods and how to take tests
- Extra time to take tests and to hand in assignments
- Alternative teaching techniques
- A private carrel for in-class work

Clearly, many of these require additional effort from the teacher, plus the extra time it takes to focus on your child's situation. I would be less than honest if I reported that this presents no problems.

In reality, there can be practical limitations to what the teacher can do for the acute needs of any one child. Here is an area where it's vital for you to establish good communication with the teacher. Ask the teacher if he feels he can accomplish the modifications and special consideration your child may need.

If the teacher replies that no, he cannot do all that should be done, ask what else he recommends.

Tutoring is one valuable option. Schools vary in their ability to provide this service. Sometimes there are before- or after-school programs, which call on a wide range of community resources, including teachers and learning specialists, qualified high school students, retired teachers and nonacademic residents with appropriate skills.

One-on-one tutoring is considered by many to be the single most effective means of intervening on behalf of a struggling student.

. . . .

Danbury, Connecticut: Coffee, Quiche, and a Busy Caseload

Child study team deliberations are an important public school process to which parents are generally not invited.

Would you like to know what goes on? Are you curious about how your child's situation will be evaluated, and what good might come of it? Here's a glimpse of one such meeting.

Place: the Hayestown Avenue School (K–5) in Danbury, Connecticut

Time: 8:30 A.M.

Setting: windowless converted storage room containing a groaning Dialta copy machine and shelves of surplus books: *Hatchet, Charlotte's Web,* a *Treasury of Literature* anthology.

Participants: a fourth-grade teacher; the music teacher; a kindergarten teacher; the psychologist; the school social worker; the resource specialist; the principal, Jose Oleveiras; and the team leader, Patti Ralabate, a speech pathologist.

Agenda: A daunting thirty "cases" to review in the four hours until lunch break.

The meeting begins with Patti setting a kitchen timer down on the formica table. Her goal, she says, is to keep the meeting moving with an average allotment of ten minutes per "case." This is met with general chuckling among the gathered teachers and staff. These meetings are famous for running overtime. In anticipation of a long morning, one teacher has arrived with coffee cake, two store-bought quiches and paper plates. Hunger will not be a factor.

Before starting, Patti briefs two substitute teachers (designated Sub A and Sub B on the intricate flow chart) who've been recruited for the specific purpose of relieving classroom teachers as they are summoned in tag-team fashion to meet with the child study team. It's never simple arranging one teacher's absence from class for even fifteen minutes, much less working out an entire morning's worth of sequential absences.

The child study team method is this: The classroom teacher summarizes her student's situation, filling in relevant background details about personality quirks, class dynamics, etc. The team then cross-examines the teacher according to their concerns and perspectives. The group then discusses remedies and possible next steps.

First up is a fifth-grade teacher who, like a candidate at a job interview, takes the empty chair facing the team. She tells about "Pedro," who she says is a good reader. "But I'm concerned about his comprehension," the teacher explains.

"What do you mean by comprehension?" a team member wants to know.

"He's more like third grade."

"How does he seem in math?"

"Grade level. The problem is just in writing. Some of his answers aren't just wrong. They're way off the mark."

The teacher is asked about Pedro's vocabulary, his spelling. He'd been in an ESL (English as second language) class until two years ago. Could his command of English be the issue?

The teacher doubts it, since there are times when his reading and writing seem fine. A team member asks the teacher if she's attempted to examine Pedro's comprehension on a sentence-by-sentence basis. Some students have trouble managing larger blocks of type (known as "chunk size").

What to do next? Everyone agrees that more detailed observation is needed. The teacher could do this if she didn't have a couple dozen other children to tend to.

Patti, who has considerable experience in this area, offers. She will set up a time to visit the class and watch the boy, possibly pull him out for a closer observation. A child who sometimes "gets it" and at other times is way off the mark is something that the team members have seen before. But the causes can be complicated.

Meanwhile, the preassigned case coordinator—in this instance, the fourth-grade teacher—will meet separately with the teacher to develop some interim strategies for improving the boy's performance.

Each case is preassigned a "case coordinator" from among the team. The underlying premise is that teachers who have recommended students for the CST are themselves asking for help. The case coordinator becomes for the teacher a co-strategist, a confidante, and a much-needed second opinion.

The morning continues. Over the next several hours, a parade of teachers present an array of cases that range from the mundane and seemingly solvable (girl catnapping in class) to the stunningly complex (bright child with severe obsessive-compulsive disorder). Each is treated by the team members with enthusiasm, seriousness, good humor, and deep concern.

Occasionally, especially in cases involving behavior problems, a team member who knows the child will chip in with information on some aspect of the child's home environment ("he's being raised by his grandparents," "her sister was in a car accident") that probably contributes. But discussion of such details is usually brief and quickly put aside.

"We try to discourage too much of that," Patti later explains. "One, it can turn into gossip and that's not fair. And two, there's nothing we can do about it. We have to stick to things we can influence."

Another teacher enters, plunks down in the vacant seat before the waiting team members. She tells of a third-grade boy who's having "extreme difficulty." He can't sit still, loses focus when he tries to read, can't seem to follow simple directions even when they are repeated. "I'm not sure what strategies to use," she says.

The teacher is told that the boy had behavior problems last year, too.

"It's not behavior," the teacher quickly counters. "He's frustrated. He wants to learn. I'm very concerned about him. I don't see him making any growth. In fact, I think he's regressing."

"How's his writing?" she's asked.

"Lots of reversals of letters."

"His reading?"

"Below primer level," is her sad reply.

Team members make silent eye contact with each other. Suspicions abound, and they clearly run in the direction of learning disabilities, possibly severe. The team recommends initiating special ed evaluation. The sooner the better.

The boy's parents will be approached by the psychologist. There's a brief discussion, since this does not always turn out the way the team hopes. On occasion, parents refuse to allow a special ed evaluation, feeling that their child will be stigmatized by the designation. Patti is insistent that the school has a professional responsibility to such children; they should do all they can to persuade the parents.

Next case, Andrew, a fifth-grade boy whose case had been heard by the CST last month.

The teacher's vivid description of Andrew's extreme organizational difficulties (loses assignment sheets minutes after they're passed out, cleans off his desk by dumping everything onto the floor) strikes an amusing chord in the team. They've all experienced versions of this many times before.

"Yesterday," the teacher reports, "Andrew complained that someone stole his pencil. 'Honey', I said, 'I don't think so.'"

That said, the teacher goes on to report that Andrew is doing markedly better. He's handing in his homework. He's up to grade level in his achievements. A strategy suggested at the previous team meeting—moving Andrew's desk to the front—has amazingly worked like a charm. He now pays far more attention in class and has done so well that the teacher recently told him he no longer needed to remain in the front. To her surprise, he chose to stay.

Andrew's future is what continues to worry the teacher. Next year is middle school, where he will shuffle between classes with no single teacher to escort him through the day. "I need to get him to start taking his own initiative," she explains, "or he's not going to make it."

People chime in with suggestions they've seen work before. Check on his organization twice every day in a way that he can expect and be prepared for. Someone recommends a book that's proven useful on instilling organization in children. Another team member urges the teacher to approach Andrew's organizational problems one task at a time rather than all at once; first his desk, for example, then his subject folders.

The teacher scribbles all this down in rapid notes, then looks up.

Recommended next step?

There's murmuring around the table, and suddenly a happy consensus. "No need for further review," Patti concludes.

The kitchen timer buzzes. For the time being, case closed.

....

Your Relationship to the Child Study Process

Schools have varying guidelines regarding the role of parents in the child study process (unlike special education processes where the parent or guardian is crucial). You will be informed that your child is being reviewed, but you are unlikely to be part of the meeting. Some questions you might want answered are:

- What will the classroom observation process be like?
- How intrusive will this be for my child?
- Will classmates know this process is occuring, and why?
- How long will it take until we know if the intervention is working?

If you are unhappy with the process, or puzzled by it, if your child is made uneasy or destabilized, or you find that your concerns are not being addressed, you should bring this to the attention of the teacher. If, for whatever reason, that is uncomfortable or if your rapport with the teacher is frayed, you should make an effort to find someone on the team (a counselor, another teacher) with whom you can communicate candidly.

Ultimately, it's important for you to feel comfortable with what the team is doing and how it is proceeding.

What Happens Next?

Essentially, the intervention will have one of three outcomes:

1. The problem will be successfully addressed. This is the goal of every child study team, and often it is achieved. End of story—except perhaps a hearty thanks to all who played a role.
2. The problem appears to have been "fixed," but in the process the team discovered an additional area of concern that will need to be further identified and explored for its underlying causes. If that is the case, your child will be introduced to a second tier of strategies tailored to the rediagnosed situation, or referred for assessment testing.
3. No significant progress has been made. Solutions were tried and nothing was accomplished. At this juncture, your child more than likely will be referred for a special education assessment (see chapter ten).

What About Testing?

Testing is not a feature of the child study process. The school will not begin assessment tests until your child is referred for a special education assessment.

Demystifying the Slow Learner

Let's face it. For some children, academic work comes easily and naturally, and for others it's nearly always an arduous, uphill climb. Teachers unquestionably know this.

Yet for a variety of reasons, rooted partly in a desire not to stigmatize the child or agitate the parent, "slow learning" is a condition that is often tiptoed around. The slow learner occupies a gray area in many classrooms, and dealing with such students is not made easier by the squeamishness surrounding the label.

In my opinion, we have come a long way from the time, not so long ago, when the term "slow learner" meant primarily one thing: Your child will never make it in school, and the sooner he or she can move on to a more congenial environment (i.e trade school or the labor force) the better.

Today, bolstered by new understandings of the multiple capacities of the human mind and, I like to think, by a more generous attitude toward the vast possibilities in store for any child who makes the effort, we are better able to view slow learners for what they truly are: children who simply learn at slower rates, and possibly in different ways.

Slow learners are not "retarded." They are not necessarily "learning disabled." Oddly, if they were, the special services offered by the school would often be substantially more than what they will otherwise receive.

Your child might at some point be designated a slow learner. You will gasp, fearing the worst. The worst being that your child is unlikely to ever grasp basic academic concepts, will suffer mightily throughout his schools years, and will not be able to go on to college and the career options that a college education can provide.

Stop! Pause! Step back and appreciate the larger picture. Because that is what the teacher and school will do.

Remember: The objective is to devise ways of helping your child, not—as might have been the case in the past—to pigeonhole or dismiss her. Your child has been designated a "slow learner" and that is a wholly manageable condition.

Maybe your initial reaction is not to stand up and cheer. But someday, you will.

What Can Be Done if Your Child Is a Slow Learner?

Keeping up will be a considerable challenge—for your child and for you.

Good teachers have many tools for making this possible. A number of these have been previously mentioned. Basically, this may entail a bit of a juggling act, trying to bolster your child's learning skills while simultaneously bringing her up to speed with the class.

Along these lines, you should ask the teacher:

- What help, during or after school, can be given?
- What specific steps will be taken to enhance your child's rate of learning?
- Will this be adequate to do the job?
- What classroom modifications will be permitted to achieve this?
- Can these be implemented in a way so your child is not stigmatized unduly?
- Are tutors available? If not at school, then where?

Dr. Mel Levine, in his book *Educational Care,* cites a sometimes overlooked quality that will ultimately be crucial in your child's ability to compensate for being a slow learner: resiliency.

Resiliency is what will allow your child to accept what might seem to be an unfair disadvantage. It will enable your child to work harder in order to accomplish the same tasks as other students. It will fortify your child when she gets only an average grade despite having outstudied higher-achieving classmates. Finally, resiliency (perseverance could be an alternate term) is what empowers your child to withstand setbacks, frustrations, and occasional failure.

Retention (Repeating the Grade)

At some point, you may be told the school is considering holding your child back a year. The teacher's reasons for making this recommendation should be fully explained to you, and you should be provided a clear sense of what is to be accomplished if this happens.

Educators are largely divided on the benefits vs. the detriments of retention. In evaluating this option, you should find out:

- Would your child repeat with the same teacher?
- What additional measures will be taken next year to avoid this year's problems?
- Would your child be horribly out of place due to age or size?
- Are there other measures, like summer school and tutoring, that can achieve as much?

There are good reasons to be cautious about such a move. Except in the early grades (K–2), there does not appear to be much conclusive evidence that children who are held back tend to significantly catch up when repeating the grade.

The Big Picture

In the United States, the belief that every child, every *person*, possesses innate skills and aptitudes is not just some lofty rhetoric for sermons and commencement addresses. It is: a) a proven fact demonstrated by countless examples of struggling students (Einstein, Edison) who hung in there long enough to make a few worthy contributions; and b) a core element in the distinctive value system we call democracy.

This belief—that every child possesses special talents and

that our country is far richer for its firm commitment to cultivating them—is central to the mission of public schools. It is the reason that the United States was the first nation in the world to undertake such a broad-scale commitment to educate all its people, and it's the reason that "leaving no child behind" must be far more than a cute phrase to teachers and school staff.

A struggling child is, therefore, the essence of a public school's mission. Quite bluntly, it's where the school does its thing.

I recognize that there is ongoing debate in the loftier reaches of academia and public policy circles about innate intelligence and the educability (or lack thereof) of some students. I realize there are those who maintain, not always overtly, that one of the ultimate functions of schools is to provide society with a massive sorting system, like professional baseball's minor leagues, saving the major league business world the expense of selecting out the best and the brightest.

But I can assure you, that is not what teachers think. Teachers are believers in the American dream, and they are believers not simply out of mushy sentimentality. We have seen over and over again the evidence. And to a remarkable degree the evidence tends to take on a familiar shape and trajectory.

It starts with that first anxious twinge of concern over a child who just doesn't seem to be able to get it. Steps are taken, interventions are applied. After months or years of hard work by the child and parent and teachers, a shift begins to occur. Not a radical transformation. Not a miracle. Just a slow, sometimes arduous process beginning to have its desired effect.

It's a process we call schooling.

BOOKS

Finding Help When Your Child Is Struggling in School
by Lawrence Greene
Solving School Problems by Elaine K. McEwan
Megaskills by Dorothy Rich

4

When Your Child Isn't Challenged

Watching your child slip into an uninspired malaise is tremendously troubling, particularly when you know that school could—*should*—be otherwise for her.

As a teacher, I found this situation to be extremely sad and also a supreme challenge. Capable students who settle for just getting by are, frankly, a mark of failure for the school, the teacher, and of course for the child.

It often surfaces first with the ubiquitous "I'm bored." Or its companion protest, "It doesn't matter." Or sometimes, with a boastful twist, "I can do it without trying." Maybe she can. But that's not good enough for your child or for you. Because, frankly, you know something about school that she does not.

You know that it's a place where vital habits can be established and lifelong patterns can be set. You know the spectacular dividends that come from having a true eagerness to learn. You know that a young mind turned properly on can stayed turned on for a lifetime. Most of all, you know that time squandered during these formative years is not easily won back.

Watching your child lapse into performing below her ability can be as unsettling as watching her fail. Because there's something else you know. Boredom is around the corner, and from there failure is not far away.

Of course there's a lot of schooling yet to go. Yes, lapses in these early years can be compensated for by later effort. No, life is not a race and school is not an Olympic competition.

But if your child is basically a good learner, if school is a place where he is well situated to thrive, then you want her engaged. Now!

Education matters. Curiosity is a quality to be cultivated like a fragile flower. Okay is not good enough. Sure, there's a chance you're making too much of this perceived slippage. But that's a risk you're willing to take.

Analyzing Your Child's Situation

The central predicament of the underchallenged student is this: The child already knows the material that is being covered in class or proceeds so rapidly through the material that she is ready to move on long before most of her classmates.

There are primarily two reasons why this would be the case:

- Your child is an advanced learner and/or possesses superior motivation
- Your child is academically gifted.

The **advanced learner** is a child who often brings to the classroom a variety of academic advantages. For starters, she may just be naturally bright. Or she may have a sibling a year or two older and as a result she's already familiar with many of the grade-level lessons. She may have a true knack for learning, and has been reading and performing basic math since the age of four. Additionally, your child's class may be large and the teacher may be focused on slower learners.

Home environment, and the emphasis parents place on education, is frequently a factor. Maybe your child gets exceptionally exposed to many forms of ambient learning, from dinner table discussions to laptop conversations with patient grandparents. Perhaps you have been diligently tutoring her in precisely those areas that the teacher covers. We all like the idea of our children getting a head start, and there are many ways—conscious and not—we try to see that it happens.

Advanced learners can also be distinguished by being very highly motivated. I don't pretend to be able to confidently generalize about the intricate psychodynamics of such children, but it does seem that the family, the extended family, and sibling rivalry can all contribute to this syndrome. In addition, some children are just plain made that way.

Gifted and **Gifted and Talented,** are terms used to denote students of exceptional ability. They apply to children who are not just smart, but *very smart*. These are children with demonstrably superior capability in areas of academic achievement or the arts, and exceptionally high IQ's.

Schools use a specific set of qualifying standards for identifying students as gifted (more on that later) and these may influence accommodations that the school will make for her. Many gifted children, however, spend their primary school years in general classrooms. Consequently, the problems they (you) face are often the same as those faced by advanced learners:

- Can the classroom remain stimulating?
- Can their learning be maintained on an upward trajectory?
- Can the teacher adapt to their special needs?
- Can the school accommodate their special needs?

Gifted learners do not necessarily share the qualities of the advanced learner. But the pace at which a gifted child absorbs and masters information, or simply seems to instinctually know and understand it, can make her equally underchallenged in the classroom.

Determining if Your Child Is Underchallenged

Tell-tale signs that your child is underchallenged can include:

- Very little studying yet average or even good grades
- Poor performance in areas of strong ability
- Sloppy and disorganized work, with no interest in improving

- Avoidance of study in subjects where he's previously shown strong interest
- Speeds through projects and assignments
- Reads extensively during class in a way that is out of synch with classmates

Some of these signs of being underchallenged are easier to detect than others. Some are quite subjective and will require discussion between you, the teacher, and maybe even the school psychologist before drawing any conclusions.

But perhaps the first thing to do is rule out the possibility of a wrong interpretation. Just because your child contends she is bored does not: a) necessarily mean that it is true, and; b) mean that being underchallenged in class is the cause.

Teachers and school psychologists report a recurring situation: parents complaining to the school that their child is "bored" when, upon further inspection, that does not seem to be true. In other words, your child's complaint at home about being bored at school might not reflect the reality of how she goes through school each day.

Certainly, your child may in fact be bored and underchallenged. But before dealing head-on with that problem, it's probably a good idea to check with the teacher. Talk to other staff. You may discover a far more upbeat and happier version of how school has been going.

As noted, you should verify that your child does indeed know much of what is being taught in the class or subject area.

Pretests try to establish what of the curriculum and current lessons is already known by a student. Pretests are available from testing companies and textbook publishers, or they can be generated by the teacher. Results of good pretests can determine if your child does indeed know much of what is to be taught and sometimes have the added virtue of pointing out gaps in the child's learning.

The catch is that only certain types of learning (grammar, basic math) can be tested in this way.

You might also ask to observe the class, to see for yourself what goes on and how your child is learning (keep in mind that parental presence is famous for altering a child's behavior). As you go about this, try to be sensitive to the potentially tricky diplomacy involved.

The underchallenged student can be a puzzlement to teachers. It may be that a complicated dynamic has developed between the teacher and your child, one that is not easy to sort out. It may turn out that the teacher is amply aware of your child's predicament and feels some guilt over not having been able to adequately address it. Remember that whatever remedies get agreed upon, they will invariably involve the teacher.

The Underachievement Syndrome

It's possible that you're wrong in your assumptions, and that your child has fallen into the more classical pattern of an **underachiever;** i.e., blaming the teacher, the curriculum, or the school for what ultimately is a personal—though no less serious—problem.

Underachievers are typically students whose academic abilities ought to place them in the upper third of a classroom but whose achievement falls far short of that. It is a syndrome that receives a lot of attention in schools, and for good reason.

Bright, underachieving kids are a challenge to teachers and parents alike. They come in all shapes and sizes. Their reasons for underachieving are as varied as the human condition itself. As a group they are characterized by many traits that are shared with underchallenged students, principally the tendency not to work up to their potential.

Where the two groups differ is largely along the lines of motivation. Underchallenged students generally wish to do well, but find themselves thwarted. Underachievers traditionally fall short on motivation, and the reasons why can sometimes be maddeningly complex.

Underachievement is a widely acknowledged syndrome within schools. Teachers and counselors are on the lookout for it. And rightly so.

This can result, I believe, in a tendency to go too far. Some children, particularly at the younger grades, are simply not ready for the challenge of competitive learning. This does not mean that they will never be ready. The so-called late bloomer is a very real phenomenon. Unfortunately, there is no way to definitively determine to whom it applies and when the longed-for blooming will occur.

I am certainly not suggesting that you sit back comfortably in the expectation that your underachieving child will undergo an eventual transformation down the road. As I've noted, an underperforming child is a serious matter. But I am cautioning against conclusively typecasting your child, or any child, especially prior to, say, fourth grade.

Kids grow and change. We wouldn't want them to be any other way.

In a similar vein, I want also to argue for the oft-overlooked integrity of the "average" student. The Garrison Keillor schtick about the Lake Woebegone school system boasting that "all of our children are above average" is both funny and a bit sad. Funny, because we are all familiar with the impulse to exaggerate the brightness of our children. Sad, because it accurately reflects our aversion to the notion of average. We so desperately want our children to be ranked above it.

I understand why that is. School is an arena where your child's future can be seriously impacted. Our children need to learn at a young age how to strive to do their best. Every parent is right to want their child to perform well.

Yet history's roster of outstanding achievers is filled with the names of "average" students. And they were not necessarily underachievers. In fact, many of them were average students who earnestly did their best, never enjoying great success, diligently earning average marks.

Then they graduated. Out in the larger world, in the competitive arenas of business and communications, the professions and the arts, where aptitudes and skills beyond sheer academic strength frequently flourish, these "average" students went on to become broadcast journalists, software engineers, screenwriters, management consultants, fashion designers, political leaders.

Remember that young students are works-in-progress. The long view, ultimately, is the one that counts.

Addressing the Teacher

If it becomes clear that your child is underchallenged in class, you must immediately involve the teacher in your concerns.

In doing this, you should pause to consider the approach you want to take. There may come a time, after other options have been explored, when the more drastic step of changing classrooms is something you may contemplate. But for now it's the teacher who will be the centerpiece of your effort. And it's with the teacher that you must forge an alliance to evaluate what's going on and to fashion some remedies.

Arrange to meet with the teacher at a convenient (and quiet) time. There's no point to beating around the bush. State your worries.

Don't be put off if you think you detect skepticism. Teachers have encountered quite a few parents who believe their children are exceptionally bright (of course, most are!). They may not always perk right up at the announcement of another one. Hang in there. Your message will get through.

Be careful not to be accusatory or confrontational. Teachers will be most interested in your concerns if they are not posed as criticism of the school or the teacher's performance. Even if you strongly feel there has been some failure, try to make your approach collaborative in spirit.

Perhaps I go too far in cautioning you. But I have seen some of these discussions get off on the wrong foot, and it's a disservice to everyone involved—you, your child, and the teacher.

You do not want the teacher to be on the defensive. You need the teacher on your side. You want an ally who shares your perspective and is uniquely able to do something about it. You will need to work closely with the teacher throughout this process.

The discussion should center on developing more insight into your child. Ask the teacher:

- Does your child in fact seem to know much of what is being taught?
- Have there been any tests or projects that reveal your child's learning level?
- If the teacher has not observed this, is there a way to make a point of doing so?
- What strategies can be used to improve the situation?
- Have these strategies worked in the past, and with what types of students?
- Are there other children in the class who share your child's learning level?

The syndrome of a bright child who chooses to slide by doing perfectly acceptable work is something that even the most astute teacher can occasionally overlook or let slide, particularly if your child is not causing any disruptions. Don't worry about seeming overly concerned or assuming an inflated idea of your child's abilities. Your attention to the problem will signal that you expect more from your child. And so should the teacher.

Yes, the teacher is also in charge of instructing twenty or more other students. Yes, there is a certain pressure on the teacher, simply as a practical matter, to gear instruction to some vague middle range of the classroom's abilities.

But that's not good enough for you or your child. And it's not good enough for most teachers. Fine-tuning all instruction to the individual needs of each child might be a logistical impossibility. But nurturing fast learners and cultivating their abilities are a point of pride with most teachers. It's a vital and exciting part of the job.

Classroom Modifications

There are many in-the-classroom strategies available for offering advanced learning opportunities to students who are beyond the regular assignment. Most of these methods are part of a trend in schools knows as "differentiation."

Differentiation attempts to work around the one-size-fits-all model. It proposes ways for teachers to adjust to students of varying abilities and achievement levels. Your child's teacher does not have to be an educational innovator or visionary in order to implement some of the methods of differentiation. (Having the time to do it is, of course, key.) The idea is simply to create instruction that can more closely fit a student's specific situation.

Some of the methods for doing this can be directed expressly for the benefit of your child, or they can be implemented class-wide. There are many such methods and teachers are constantly developing new ones, especially as the call for differentiation accelerates.

Some common ones are:

- *Curriculum compacting* attempts to give students credit through a process of pretesting for material they already know and allowing them to move on to the next level. Or allowing students of exceptional ability to move more rapidly through the material.
- *Enrichment* activities should fill the surplus time enjoyed by students who are exempted from normal class work because they already know the material. Teachers can be creative in developing such options, and the work should allow students to elaborate on what they've just learned. For example, a student who has already mastered the class list of spelling words can proceed on to a writing project using the designated words.

- *Flexible (or cluster) grouping* matches students by their needs, interests, abilities, and readiness to handle projects, not neccesarily by age. In effect, this is a method of incorporating some of the principles of tracking, except there is easy and frequent mobility for students moving from one group to another.

    Fourth graders, for example, can be grouped to move through content areas (Ancient Egypt, fractions) at differing rates of progress, with a more advanced group undertaking more challenging material.

- *Tiered assignments* are lessons that allow students to explore ideas in a way that builds on prior knowledge. More motivated or capable students can thus move on to more challenging facets of the exercise.

- *Learning centers* are a way of structuring the physical space within a classroom, allowing groups of students to work simultaneously on different assignments at varying achievement levels.

- *Independent study* where the teacher creates special projects or long-term assignments related to the curriculum for students to investigate.

- *Parallel curriculum* is a somewhat innovative teaching method that allows students to learn the same material along different tracks more tailored to their learning level. Thus, an underchallenged student might be given above grade-level reading materials that are nonetheless consistent with the topic being studied.

- *Learning logs* are journals teachers assign which call on students to record in detail what they are learning and to reflect on it. These can be a device for your child to expand on what is being taught and to add an additional level of challenge.

- *Homework* is another chance for the teacher to offer your child more challenging assignments. Enhanced homework assignments can signal your child that the teacher appreciates her advanced learning level and is eager to address it.

In summary, there's plenty that can be done. Your child's contention that she already knows what's being taught is far from the end of the discussion. There's always a further level of exploration that can be introduced.

Obviously, you would not want your child to feel burdened by these additional challenges. Kids, by and large, do not like the idea of more work. Thus, where possible, these "extra" projects should be compensated for by some exemptions like, for example, release from rehashing material she already knows.

Bowling Green, Kentucky: Talent Scouts

With considerable anxiety, Helen Gallagher enrolled her daughter Jamie for third grade in Cumberland Trace Elementary School. After three years at another local school, Jamie was being forced by redistricting to switch.

But the reason for her fears went deeper than the standard discomfort at starting anew among strangers. In truth, Jamie's situation had not been all that happy at her old school.

A bright child with a precocious capacity to learn, especially in the language arts, Jamie had found first and second grades to be a sea of frustration. An early reader, she'd found herself bored having to read books that were severely beneath her level. Being asked to repetitively practice spelling words which she'd long ago mastered made her irritable and obstinate. At one point, Helen feared for her daughter's mental health.

Before this new school year began, Helen arranged to meet with Cumberland Trace's principal, Mary Evans.

Helen's objective was to brief the new school on Jamie's academic brightness and the dilemmas this presented. Helen was not, however, optimistic. In earlier grades, she'd had several such meetings with the old school and found that there was little they were able to do.

Second grade in particular had gone from bad to worse. Much of the work Jamie was assigned turned out to be material she'd been given by her first grade teacher who was trying to keep her challenged. Eventually Jamie refused to do homework and became disruptive. The principal advised skipping Jamie a grade, but Helen worried that her daughter was not socially prepared to be with older children. "Her mood," recalls Helen, "was terrible."

At that initial meeting at Cumberland Trace, Helen had one main question: Was there anything, anything at all, that the school could do to make academic work more stimulating for her daughter?

Mary Evans turned out to be the light at the end of the tunnel. A former teacher of gifted education, she was in her sixth year as principal of Cumberland Trace. Around the time Mary took over as principal, the community decided to conduct a school survey, which revealed a large concern over children who were not being challenged. Correcting that problem had became a central part of Mary's mission.

In Mary's analysis, there are primarily three reasons why schools may fail to serve some of their more capable students.

First is time. In busy classrooms that encompass a wide range of abilities, the brighter kids are often the easiest to ignore.

Second, teachers are not usually trained to work in a differentiated way with students of varying levels.

Third, administrators don't always demand that teachers adjust to students of varying levels.

All of these, Mary vowed, would be addressed at Cumberland Trace. On taking over, she immediately arranged workshops for teachers that focused on strategies for differentiation. "Teachers should think of themselves as talent scouts," she explains. To that end, Mary set about reshaping the school climate to emphasize respect for achievement and recognition of the different types of abilities.

Every morning at Cumberland Trace begins with a school-wide assembly in the gymnasium. Several hundred youngsters pile off the buses and proceed to the gym where they all take a seat and quietly read together for fifteen minutes. It's known as the "Get Caught Reading" period.

Then Mary steps to the microphone.

"Why did you come to school today?" she calls out.

"To learn as much as we can," the children all reply in unison, as they do every day.

"How do we do that?" she asks.

"By doing quality work," they enthusiastically reply.

Helen recalls that first meeting. "Mary assured me that they would take care of Jamie." Unlike empty assurances of the past, Mary Evans was able to explain exactly how this would be accomplished.

From morning assembly right through the day, Cumberland Trace is structured to encourage differentiation. The "Talent Development Plan," a program of individualized enrichment activities which the state of Kentucky mandates for gifted children, is widely used at Cumberland Trace throughout all grades. Children are taught—and teachers are trained to teach—according to children's developmental level, not age level.

"I *don't teach* third grade," explains teacher Emily Duryea. "I *work with* third graders."

How does this function?

Teachers give their classes pretests. These are done at the start of the year, and periodically throughout, for the purpose of determining what children already know, and do not know. Based on the results of the pretests, students are then grouped with others of similar needs.

Emily Duryea's math class works roughly like this: Children sit at four long tables. As kids busily apply themselves to work sheets (which differ from child to child, according to their learning level), Emily calls out the names of seven children who rise and come forward to assemble on a tiered wooden riser above where Emily sits.

(Years ago, before Mary's tenure, a handy parent with carpentry skills had built several such constructions for the school. With seating capacity for a half dozen or so children, the risers ideally accomodate the small group clusters that are the heart and soul of differentiated instruction.)

With these students, Emily reviews the problems they should be tackling in the math book and answers questions students have about the work they've encountered. ("A number divided by itself always equals one," she tells one boy.)

This review lasts perhaps ten minutes. Then Emily sends these children back to their tables, and calls aloud the names of five more children. "Math class can look like a circus," she admits, "but if a circus works, it's a good thing."

Emily estimates that the learning range within this class is approximately one and a half years. Teaching this way—sorting children via pretests, addressing their needs in flexible groups—enables her to cater to the needs of slower learners while creating challenges for more advanced students. The same process occurs with reading and social studies.

Though children do have some idea that they are grouped according to achievement level, there is no special status or privilege associated with a "higher" group. "Fun" and special projects are assigned to each group, not just the more advanced learners, according to Todd Otto, a fifth-grade teacher.

There is considerable opportunity for children to move from group to group, and not always upward. If pretests determine that a child knows much of what his group is about to tackle, he may be moved to a more challenging group. If a child is struggling, the team (consisting of the two or three teachers) will caucus and possibly recommend a "lower" group placement.

All this is done with a minimum of fanfare. When parents ask which group their child is placed in, they are told without intent to be evasive, "your child is placed in a group that meets his needs."

For Jamie Gallagher, this was just what the doctor ordered. At the start of each week, her class is given a pretest covering the upcoming vocabulary words. In this way, she can demonstrate that she's mastered the words, along with their correct spelling. Now, however, she is neither left to languish nor consigned to a perpetual rehash. Instead, Jamie is encouraged to select her own vocabulary list and to work on that alongside her classmates.

If a week's list consists of words with, for example, long e's, or short a's, or atypical vowel combinations, the vocabulary list Jamie selects from the dictionary must contain those elements. Such independent words recently selected by Jamie include: latitude, malaise, formidable, and accessible. When Jamie presents her list, the teacher asks her to provide the page number from the dictionary where each word was found.

Sure, it involves more work. But according to her mother, Jamie isn't complaining. "It empowers her to think she has a say-so," reports Helen. "She loves it!"

....

What's the Truth About Tracking?

Tracking, or ability grouping, is the name for the practice of aggregating students in classrooms according to their perceived achievement levels. The practice has been reduced or eliminated in some elementary schools, at least in its overt form. It exists in middle schools in various ways and more so in high schools.

The predicament that tracking sets out awkwardly to address remains one of the greatest challenges facing teachers: how to manage instruction in the classroom to meet the needs of children with a wide range of abilities and aptitudes? What books to use? What assignments to give? How to find a rigorous yet fair common denominator?

The benefits of tracking are thought to be:

- Enabling faster learners to proceed at a pace unimpeded by slower learners
- Allowing struggling students to learn at a more accommodating pace without comparing themselves to faster learners
- Allowing teachers to focus their efforts to suit a more homogeneous group, sharpening their efforts

Critics of the practice, such as Jeannie Oakes, point out that:

- Average and slower students do not benefit from it.
- Slower students are stigmatized before they have had a chance to develop academically.

- Despite the claim of protecting them from unflattering peer measurements, slower students lose self-esteem and underperform when placed in lower tracked classes.

In recent years, tracking has been partially supplanted by the practice of "flexible grouping," clustering students by achievement in specific subject areas, like math and reading, for parts of the day. Many teachers employ some form of grouping in reading. They offer, for example, less advanced readers simpler books that suit their abilities while giving better readers the chance to tackle more difficult projects. The practice is also used, although less widely, in math.

Complementing this is a practice called "streaming," whereby advanced students in, say, math can move to another grade level solely for that subject area.

You should ask your child's teacher or the principal how the school implements flexible grouping, if at all. You will want to know:

- At what grade does this begin? (*It can occur as early as kindergarten.*)
- How are decisions made, and who is involved? (*Usually the decision is made by the teacher, sometimes with input from a reading or math specialist.*)
- Are teacher assignments made with grouping in mind? (*Usually not.*)
- Will you be notified if your child is grouped? (*Probably not. This is considered an internal matter that the teacher prefers not to call attention to.*)
- Can a student ever switch to a different group? (*Definitely, and this frequently occurs.*)
- Are these groupings part of your child's written record? (*They should not be.*)

Out-of-Classroom Possibilities

There are several options outside the classroom for your child to find additional challenges.

Tutors are normally thought of as back-up resources for students who are having trouble. But your school has the capability of finding a tutor, mentor, or resource specialist to work with your advanced child. Clearly, your child would have to be willing to have this relationship and your child's teacher would have to figure out a nondisruptive way for this to work.

Clubs and after-school groups are a common way for schools to develop challenging academic opportunities that go beyond the classroom. Some examples are math clubs, science clubs, and book groups.

Often run by parent volunteers, perhaps overseen by teachers, these programs try to blend enhanced learning with stimulating games and competition. What schools offer in this regard depends largely on the willingness and availability of volunteers; programs which don't exist now may be initiated next semester.

If you have the time, establishing such an academic club with the cooperation of other parents and school staff can prove a great way to make sure your child remains engaged in learning. To find out more about how this can be done, consult with school officials or your local parent-teacher organization.

If it's any consolation, you should know that educators report that the phenomena of underchallenged students is far more prevalent in the years K–3.

Starting in fourth grade, students encounter more varied and complex problem-solving approaches to curriculum, and far fewer rote exercises. Complaints about being underchallenged drop off substantially from then on.

What is Gifted Education?

"Gifted" or "gifted and talented" is the term ascribed to students of exceptional ability. It is meant to apply to children who are not just smart, but *very smart*. Many schools try to establish separate programs for these children, realizing that a regular classroom may leave them, at least in some subject areas, significantly underchallenged.

Sounds simple enough, doesn't it? Well, sometimes it is. But there can be complications.

Eligibility decisions can prove contentious. Adequate funding is a problem in many districts. Plus, some schools don't even consider such programs for fear of appearing to give special treatment to certain students.

This should not be the case. Gifted and talented programs are not about elitism. Gifted children deserve no less than other groups of exceptional and special needs children: namely, an appropriate learning environment.

Parents of gifted children are quick to point out that this reluctance to grant special treatment does not apply—nor should it—to the learning disabled or physically challenged. Why stint in programs for children who are also far removed from the classroom mainstream?

Part of the reason for this is the abiding belief that high achieving learners are, generally speaking, not really a problem. Because the dilemmas of accelerated learners seem somehow less desperate than, say, those of children falling behind, schools can slip into the habit of paying less attention to them. Thus, it has been referred to as "the quiet crisis."

And crisis is not too strong a word for it. For the average classroom can turn into a quicksand of frustrations for a gifted child.

Determining if Your Child is "Gifted"

Determining giftedness, and thereby ascertaining eligibility for formal school programs, is not an exact science.

Nonetheless, educators in the field (and parents of gifted and talented children) maintain that meaningful and measurable distinctions do exist. They cite a range of exceptional qualities (extensive use of complex vocabulary at an early age, intense immersion in projects, rapid processing of information, etc.) which in and of themselves may not clearly constitute giftedness, but in combination with results from one or more standard ability (I.Q.) tests can certify that your child qualifies.

Schools employ different standards for determining giftedness. Most tend to have a multistage process for identifying and selecting gifted students eligible for programs that look something like this:

- Parent application
- Standard achievement test
- Teacher nomination
- I.Q. test

It is generally recognized that the best evaluator of whether a child is exceptionally advanced tends to be you, the parent. If you believe your child falls into this category, you should bring it to the attention of the teacher and school.

Standards tests are a preliminary tool used by many school districts for screening students eligible for special or gifted programs.

In making selections for gifted programs, teachers are also urged to search for:

1. *Motivational characteristics.* Is your child active in class discussions, eager to do extra work, and capable of working independently?
2. *Creativity.* Is your child a strong problem solver, a risk taker? Does her work show originality?
3. *Learning characteristics.* Is your child quick to grasp new concepts? Does she show advanced vocabulary and consistently high performance?

There are bound to be shifts and reevaluations of the working definition of "giftedness" as schools seek additional ways of serving this part of their population. Whereas gifted programs often require measurable criteria for determining eligibilty, it's good to remember that no such cut-off marks exist in nature.

What Programs Exist at Your Child's School?

The school principal and psychologist should be able to provide you with detailed information about what the school has to offer. You should learn, with some specificity, what the school would like to accomplish by affording your child these services.

Special education for gifted learners takes several basic forms, with budget and personnel being the determining features.

Gifted resource or **pull-out programs** provide a way for advanced learners to spend special time with their peers in the presence of a teacher dedicated to their needs. Studies have shown that advanced learners greatly benefit, psychologically as well as educationally, from exposure to their peers in an isolated setting. In such situations, they are more likely to undertake more challenging projects.

Typically, these pull-out groups consist of three to six children. Sessions can be scheduled as often as several times per week or as few as once per week, depending on resources.

Acceleration is school system jargon for what was formerly known as "skipping." Due to the complex psychological effects on the child, this option is exercised only with caution. Acceleration can nonetheless be helpful when a child is learning at a rate markedly faster and with greater depth than peers.

Typically, your child is considered eligible for acceleration if on standard tests she scores two or more grade levels beyond where she is assigned.

In considering whether to accelerate your child, you should consult the school psychologist, principal, and teacher. The benefits for certain advanced learners are quite pronounced, but the child must be mature enough to withstand the possible social awkwardness.

Single subject acceleration is a partial version of the above, geared toward subject areas where the child has exceptional abilities. Single subject acceleration is more readily approved by administrators and teachers than blanket acceleration.

Making the Normal Classroom More Challenging

Most of the accommodations mentioned above in reference to underchallenged students can be effectively employed with gifted children.

Regrettably, most classroom teachers have not had much formal training in ways to handle gifted learners. The vast disparity in abilities contained in an average elementary classroom, particularly large ones, can be staggering. In such situations, the needs of a gifted child can get ignored.

As Theresa Staples, the 2000 Gifted and Talented Association Teacher of the Year from Carrollton, Georgia, explains, "Let's be realistic. Here you have a child who can read properly and do complex math, and over here you have a child who can barely read at all. As a teacher, where are you going to put your energy?"

There are also some gifted learners whose abilities are so extraordinary that reasonable options are hard to come by in the normal classroom. Last year, for example, at a community meeting in Ames, Iowa, to discuss gifted education, a father in the audience stood up to ask the panel of five experts a question about his daughter.

She was, the father stated, in the first grade and very advanced. So advanced that she was feeling strange about herself and growing alienated from other students. "What," the father wanted to know, "can the school do to improve this situation?"

"Exactly how advanced," inquired a panel member, "is your daughter?"

With not a hint of boastfulness, the father explained, "She is in the first grade and has tested in the 99th percentile for fifth graders for math."

The panel members stared at each other in silence.

After regaining their composure, several panelists eagerly offered an array of suggestions—tutors from the nearby university, enrichment programs on Saturdays at a nearby museum, play dates with one or two other gifted children.

The father listened patiently, politely. Then he sat down. There was no need to remark on the obvious: None of the suggestions involved the classroom or the school. The reality was, and often is, that with an exceedingly gifted child, there is only so much that can be done in a normal classroom and a regular school.

The Big Picture

I'm not the sort of teacher who's been fixated on test scores or grade outcomes. I have been known in my time to give an appropriate reward to the slower child who did his darndest, and to criticize a higher achiever who loafed. I believe—rather, *I know*—that learning is a process, not a contest.

As a parent, I was acutely aware that what truly mattered was having my daughters, to borrow a phrase from youth culture, "turned on" to learning. In this, schools must take a primary responsibility.

It is the school's job to teach information and learning skills. But a crucial component of that job is to stimulate and inspire students to go as far as possible. Some teachers are able to do it with winning personalities and imaginative techniques. Some are able to do it by crafting intriguing assignments and through an artful approach to the subject matter.

There may come a time, as discussed, when you feel your child is not being well served in this respect. If that occurs, the school needs to step up and take heed. The fact that your child is far from failing is not good enough.

Leave no child behind is a popular slogan—and a good one—used by President Bush and other politicians to express their desire to improve learning throughout our schools, even for those students who have been traditionally lagging.

Leave no child underchallenged could be its equally urgent companion slogan.

WEBSITES

The National Association for Gifted Children *www.nacg.org*
Hoagie's Gifted Education Page *www.hoagiesgifted.org*
National Research Center on the Gifted and Talented
www.gifted.uconn.edu/

5

Approaching Homework: What You Should Do and How to Keep the Experience Sane

Your goals, on the face of it, are simple enough. You want your child to comply with the assignments and you want to be there to help if help is needed.

End of story? You wish.

There are probably households where homework is no big deal. For others, many others, homework presents a lot of complications.

Your child may be confused concerning what is expected, and the importance of it. You may be similarly confused, or at least incompletely informed. You hear of teachers who assign two hours' worth per night, and others who rarely assign any. You hear of parents who participate as a virtual collaborator alongside their child, and others who play no role whatsoever. You don't know what's right or fair and you're not even sure what is best for your child.

That's why the experience is increasingly known by the not-altogether exaggerated phrase, *The Homework Wars*. In many families, homework turns into a nightly tussle that is a source of ongoing anxiety and displeasure to child and parent alike. So why do homework at all?

Because to most educators and the majority of parents, homework is an essential means of supplementing classroom learning. It encourages the development of knowledge and skills that cannot always be sufficiently handled during the course of the school day, and it affords parents a glimpse into the work habits and achievement level of their child.

Proponents of homework (few of whom are school children) believe that as we come to live increasingly in a global economy that prizes an educated and skilled work force, we owe it to our children to provide them a leg up on the inevitable competition. Even if doing so extends each day's schoolwork into overtime.

Homework advocates, such as Janine Bempechat, a Harvard University professor of education, point out there is also nonacademic value in take-home assignments. Teaching young children to budget their free time, exercise self-discipline in pursuit of larger objectives, to cultivate responsibility and exercise diligence are well worth the inconveniences.

These "inconveniences," of course, are what gives rise to the battle. They can include highly stressed children juggling an assortment of after-school activities, highly stressed parents juggling an array of work and family responsibilities, plus a daily household schedule that seemingly needs to be managed with militaristic punctuality.

Is it worth it? I believe it is. But like so many aspects of parenting, it is hard to separate the issue at hand from the values you bring to the discussion. Do you want your child to be a high achiever or merrily contented? Would you prefer your child to be self-disciplined or carefree? Do you strive for a happy blend? Can that be achieved?

When conflict and misunderstandings occur between parents and schools—and rest assured, this one is heating up—I try to look for a missing piece. Is there some aspect of the discussion that is being overlooked?

With homework, it might be this: Are we clear about the goal of it? Are all the stakeholders in agreement? Is there a clear understanding of why homework is assigned, what it is designed to accomplish, what it means when a child performs it successfully, or fails to do so?

These aren't easy questions, and I do not pose them to frustrate you. But the topic of homework will likely be part of the running dialogue you participate in as a public school parent. Any understanding you can achieve will serve you well.

How to Know What Your Child is Expected to Do

At one point or another, you'll probably have reason to be skeptical about some homework-related contention made by your child. Homework is an arena famous for misunderstandings, mixed messages, and, frankly, misinformation. Whose fault this ultimately is remains another subject altogether.

I believe that it is the teacher's job to communicate this unified sense of homework. Ideally, teachers should explain their homework policies to parents at a start-of-the-year open house or curriculum night.

But teachers do not always do this, or at least they do not always do this successfully. And even if these sessions are offered, parents do not always attend.

If "fogginess" is a regular feature of your encounter with homework, you should either meet with the teacher or have a telephone conversation. It is appropriate for you to ask:

- Is there a way to improve communication about the assignments?
- What are the goals for homework assignments?
- Should your child be able to manage the assignments without help, or is it assumed that an adult will pitch in?
- How much time, roughly speaking, should the assignments take?
- Does failure to perform the assignments suggest academic problems?

For homework to be productive, it is important for you, your child, and the teacher to have a good understanding of an assignment's:

- Academic purpose (What skill is it developing?)
- Requirements and expectations
- Anticipated time allotment
- Importance in relation to curriculum goals (How does it fit? Where does it contribute to the learning objective?)
- Importance in relation to grade or evaluation

Confusion about homework—its substance, aims and intents—can present a serious problem. And when vagueness of purpose and direction is added to the myriad environmental complications (such as household distractions and conflicted demands for time), even a diligent student can be swiftly undermined.

Are Your Child's Homework Assignments Useful and Appropriate?

Good homework assignments should:

- Be clear and manageable
- Be goal-directed, i.e. clearly connected to ongoing classroom objectives
- Be consistent with your child's achievement level
- Encourage thinking and problem-solving

Bad homework assignments:

- Are a repetition of exercises done in class
- Vary greatly in intensity and amount
- Are significantly above or below your child's level
- Are impossible to do without adult participation
- Are used as punishment
- Contain unreasonable expectations

How Much Help Should You Give?

The dilemma of parental overinvolvement in homework was cleverly expressed in a *New Yorker* magazine cartoon depicting a child standing before the stern teacher in the classroom. The child's face displays that hangdog look of guilt. "I can't hand in my homework," the child sheepishly explains in the caption, "because my parents didn't do it."

Most parents have experienced some version of this dilemma. It's a contorted little dance that you may be familiar with. Your child labors at the kitchen table over a hand-out sheet. You glance over his shoulder, just to see what's going on.

It's math, and to your untrained eye it appears as though your child has some of the problems wrong. You hover nearby to inspect what he does next. It's a long division problem. Ouch! He got that one wrong, too.

Here's a quick quiz for you: What *should* you do?

Second quiz question: What *did* you do?

Parents definitely have a role to play regarding homework. For starters, it is an excellent means of getting acquainted with what your child is learning and the expectations being set by the teacher.

I am a firm believer that parents should always be aware that **uninvolvement** sends the message that either you are too busy to be concerned or you don't think it's important.

Overinvolvement likewise risks negative side effects. The most obvious is that problems solved with excessive parental assistance undermine your child's ability to confidently master the material. Similarly, a child with too much adult help can fail to fully cultivate the self-discipline and resourcefulness that is an important piece of the homework experience.

Appropriate involvement is when the adult is:

- Situated nearby, without being involved in every question or problem

- Supportive and encouraging, not critical
- Informed (at least minimally) about the assignment and the subject matter
- Respectful of the assignment, restrained in criticisms of it

It helps to be alert to the routine ways children fall into homework difficulty. They:

- Are not aware that an assignment has been given
- Do not understand the assignment or come away with an inaccurate description of it
- Fail to bring the necessary book, folder, or page home
- Don't allot enough time to do the assignment
- Leave long term projects until the last minute
- Fail to check and review the work
- Forget to bring the work to school
- Allow the dog to eat it (just kidding!)

Keep in mind that if you can avoid having homework turn into the vaunted war, it can actually prove to be a remarkably rich learning exercise, and not just for your child. You may gain insights into how your child learns (a key factor in his ongoing academic development—see Chapter 6 about learning differences) and learn better what you do not know (and should) to assist your child's education.

If your child is experiencing academic problems, you may want to take additional measures, like tutoring. Completing your child's homework for him is not, however, a productive option.

Special reports and long-term projects are another tricky area. These more complex assignments, which are often intended by the teacher to require your help and guidance, offer a tremendous opportunity to help your child learn a detailed subject. They also present an outstanding opportunity for overparticipation and abuse.

Because projects of this nature are often eventually put on display for the entire class, and sometimes the entire school, children (and parents) are eager to show their best. And my, do some of those displays look great!

History reports replete with Madison Avenue graphic representations. Science results with intricate motorized demonstrations. Three-dimensional dioramas that would look good in the Museum of Natural History.

Obviously, new developments in educational technology make it possible for today's students to make a far more polished presentation than was imaginable just a few short years ago. Part of the reason teachers who work closely with new technologies are so enthusiastic about them is for the ways these can motivate students to purse greater achievements.

But you know what I'm getting at. There is a proper level for your involvement, and it hovers somewhere—sorry for the vagueness here—between all and nothing. Nobody is going to tell you where that delicate balance exists.

It's your job, and your child's, to figure it out. It may vary from task to task, and from subject area to subject area. There will be times when your child needs more assistance, and times when, thank you, none is needed at all. There will be times, frankly, when you're just not up to it.

Always remember the long range goal: Eventually your child needs to stand on his own and say, I can do it!

. . . .

Relevant Fact

A University of Michigan study comparing homework loads between 1981 and 1997 found the amount had almost tripled for six- to nine-year-olds.

. . . .

How Much Time Should Your Child Be Spending on Homework (and How Much Is Too Much?)

The NEA along with the national PTA suggests as a rule-of-thumb a homework load of ten minutes per night per grade level. A third grader would thus be assigned an estimated thirty minutes of homework, sixty minutes for a sixth grader, not to exceed two hours per night in high school.

Clearly, any attempt to prescribe a standard amount would be constraining to teachers and families. Exceptions abound. What about extracurricular reading? Science fairs? Math clubs? And of course there is the issue of time to learn from after-school activities, such as music, sports, and scouting.

Reacting to the community's sense that homework was impinging on extracurricular activities, Verne Ash, a middle school principal from Chesterton, Indiana, created a forty-five-minute period each day after lunch where students, pressed for time, can do their homework. "So many kids are involved in so many things after school, " says Ash. "We do what we can not to burden them with work that is meaningless."

It is appropriate, and often necessary, for parents to create individualized homework requirements to their child. What one child can accomplish in a nifty ten minutes might take another child a rigorous forty-five.

Similarly, in creating homework assignments teachers must be sensitive to the fact that the assignment might find one child breezing through in ten minutes and another laboring for over an hour. There is really no way around this disparity.

The key to adjusting the fit is communication between you and the teacher.

Parents concerned that homework assignments are requiring either too much time, or too little, should:

- Find out from the teacher how long the assignment is meant to take
- Convey to the teacher how your child's experience differs from that
- See if assignments can be reduced to essential elements if your child is spending an excessive amount of time
- See if assignment can be enlarged (through exercises that broaden, not just multiply, the work load) if your child is spending too little time

One of the biggest problems that parents and students experience with homework is inconsistency.

Increases in homework should be incremental and predictable. Wild fluctuations in homework amounts, either week to week or grade to grade, should be brought to the attention of the teacher or the principal. Your child should not, for example, have intensive homework in fourth grade and a drastic drop-off in fifth grade.

You don't need to be reminded that your child's academic development is a work-in-progress, to be cultivated wisely and cautiously. And the school should not need to be reminded of this either.

•••

Asheville, North Carolina: Starting Young

As a veteran kindergarten teacher, Lois Jones is keenly aware of the stunned look of amazement that crosses the faces of parents when she announces at the start of the school year that their five- to six-year-old child, only recently weaned from afternoon naps, is going to be regularly assigned homework.

Homework in kindergarten?

Lois empathizes with the parents' bewilderment. Part of her wishes homework was not required. She wishes she could be utterly free to teach the students in the relaxed, flowing and creative way that comes so naturally to her.

But Lois has learned that even in kindergarten, the system has expectations, and there are consequences to ignoring them.

Lois recalls her first year teaching kindergarten (she'd previously taught high school and middle school, in her words, "working my way down, down, down to where I belong"). Homework was the furthest thing from her mind.

At the start of her second kindergarten year, she was unexpectedly confronted by several of last year's kids scampering over to her room, begging to return to her class, clinging to her and crying, "please don't make me go back there" (first grade).

The problem was not that the new first-grade teacher was nasty or uncaring or overly demanding. It was that Lois' students were not used to taking assignments home and returning to school with the work completed. They were not used to the classtime discipline of staying at their desks for sustained stretches of time and working silently.

"They weren't ready," Lois recalls. "I was traumatized, truly traumatized, that I had not properly prepared them."

The conclusion Lois Jones came to was that homework—yes, even in kindergarten—plays an indispensable role in the preparation of children for future school experiences. Why that has come to pass is, perhaps, an interesting question (reasons cited most often are the dire 1983 National Commission on Excellence in Education report, *A Nation at Risk* and, though it's hard to grasp now, an early 1980s drive to keep up with the highly educated Japanese). But it's not a question so interesting that Lois, or her kindergartners, will get sidetracked from their mission.

The state of North Carolina recommends for kinder-gartners homework assignments amounting to 30 min-utes or less per evening. Lois has developed two basic programs for achieving this.

One she calls a "share box." This is a modified show-and-tell where students bring to class an item from home that is consistent with the week's theme—the color red, for example. The child writes out a label for the item (a red stuffed animal?), prepares something to say about this object, and then answers questions from other children about why this object was picked, where it came from, etc.

Lois' goal is to get children comfortable with present-ing information in front of their peers, to make home part of the child's educational experience, and to establish work habits they can use later in their schooling.

"Homework," says Lois, "should be additional practice for something you're doing in the classroom, but a differ-ent way of doing it. I try to create homework that will give parents an indication of how their child is doing."

Not all parents are delighted. Some are too busy to regularly sit down to the tasks. Others question the worth of such seemingly basic exercises. It's no mystery why the concept of homework for kindergartners is grating for many parents. It flies in the face of what many believe is appropriate for their young child and it contrasts harshly with their fond memories of their own early school experiences.

Lois Jones sympathizes. Acquainting kindergartners, however superficially, with the rigors of curricular achieve-ment was not her idea. She continues to worry that in the frenzy of intensifying academic pressure, the "whole child" might sometimes get lost.

But if Lois ever has doubts about starting kinder-gartners promptly on this path, she need only remind herself of her initial kindergarten trauma. "I promised myself then," she recalls, "that next year, my children would be prepared. It didn't matter if I agreed with it or not. Children should not be placed in a position where they feel incompetent."

....

What If You Don't Understand the Subject Matter (i.e. Do You Need to Learn This Stuff, Too?)

Ah yes, what to do when your child, mired in frustration on a math problem or history report, pleads for your help. You eagerly step up, only to stare over his shoulder in clueless, bug-eyed incomprehension.

Do you:

a) Based on your superior wisdom and experience, take a wild stab at the answer?
b) Based on your dim recollection of having done quite well in this subject during your own school years, take a wild stab at the answer?
c) Dash to another room to place telephone calls to friends, thumb frantically through resource books, or access internet websites, then take a stab at the answer?
d) Confess ignorance?

There is nothing wrong, in my opinion, with declaring that you simply do not know the answer. Indeed, there were many evenings with my daughters when I did not fully understand the question. What you should be careful not to do is criticize the assignment. Any complaints you might have in this regard should be raised separately, and privately, with the teacher.

I should also point out that this predicament of being stumped alongside your child can be a marvelous *teachable moment*.

Walking your child through the steps you take to get the correct answers when you, too, are stumped—breaking a problem down into simpler parts, augmenting your knowledge by consulting other resources, etc.—can be immensely instructive.

It can also lead your child to holler out in frustration, "Just give me the answer!"

In which case, you have reentered the homework wars.

Sorting Through Evasions and Excuses

Avoiding homework or falsely creating the impression it has already been completed are age-old specialties of schoolchildren, sometimes inspiring them to feats of creativity and inventiveness rarely evidenced . . . well, in their homework.

Knowing this long and rich tradition, you should be vigilant.

It would, of course, be nice if your relationship to your child was one of perfect candor and responsiveness. It would be nice if when you asked, "Did you do your homework?", the answer was straightforward and forthright. For those of you who enjoy such a relationship with your child, this section may be irrelevant.

The rest of you understand that your child's behavior around homework periodically merits at least a second glance.

Most teachers adhere to a routine homework policy (how often it will be assigned, what they expect) and they so inform the class. If your child does not convey this information to you, it is easy and appropriate for you to get it from the teacher. Just ask. It's good information to have.

Teachers make a practice of regular weekday assignments. Some, however, assign only sporadically or at times of particular significance (field trips, special projects). If your child continually says he has no homework, it wouldn't hurt to double check with the teacher. Even if your child appears to be keeping pace, it might still be a good idea to occasionally ask the teacher if that is the case.

Students who become delinquent in their homework assignments run the risk of hurting their grade, sometimes past the point of no return. It's important for you and your child to know what the teacher's policy is regarding making up for missed assignments, i.e. can it be done? What are the extended deadlines for getting it done?

What Can Homework Teach You About Your Child?

Finally, homework is your chance to see for yourself how your child is doing. To put it bluntly, you lose a golden opportunity if you decline to play or feel you are too busy to play a role in your child's homework.

The insights you gain by closely observing your child perform academic work can be a valuable supplement to the school's understanding of your child, and how she learns. Sure, you could say that this is the teacher's job. But the important subtleties of how your child learns, how he processes information (or fails to), whether, for example, math errors are the result of sloppiness or incomprehension, might elude a teacher with twenty or more other children to attend to.

What can you look for?

1. Attentional issues. Does your child work well by doing the work in a straight block of time, or is she easily distracted and in need of frequent breaks?
2. Subject matter strengths and weaknesses. Does your child approach some subjects more readily than others? Do some areas confound your child? Do some subjects come to her with almost instinctual ease?
3. Subject matter interest (not always the same as above). Is there a curiosity for some subjects that lingers beyond the bounds of the homework assignment?
4. Disparities between school reports (grades) and what you observe.
5. Self-confidence, or lack of it.
6. Learning differences. Does your child prefer graphic rep-

resentations of math problems? Does she prefer to practice spelling words while walking around? (see Chapter 6.)

7. Learning disability, especially some of the subtler types. Is there inconsistency in reading comprehension? Does she have an aversion to large chunks of text?

The better teachers understand that you are immensely valuable to your child's education, that you are, in effect, your child's first teacher. In that capacity, you must do what good teachers do: try your best to understand how your child learns. Homework is the place to start.

The Big Picture

The ongoing debate over homework, like other issues I've explored, presents us with an opportunity to step back, dust off our glasses, adjust our perspective, take a breath, and see if there isn't a way to focus a bit more clearly.

What do we want our children to become?

> Skilled? Yes.
> Informed? Without question.
> Disciplined and persistent? Certainly.
> Goal-oriented? Yes.
> Driven? Hmmm, depends on what that means.
> Single-minded? I don't think so.
> Obsessive and one dimensional? Definitely not!

The homework debate as currently constructed exposes the often contradictory attitudes that parents have about their children. We want them to be spontaneous and happy. We want them also to be motivated and successful. Homework is where these twin wishes collide.

There is no ultimate right or wrong way. If we knew unequivocally what was best, I am reasonably confident we would be doing it. I firmly believe that homework can play an extremely positive role in a child's development of sound work habits as well as academic achievement.

As a practical matter, however, choices need to be made by parents and teachers and children in the face of competing objectives.

Choices about homework get regularly made by schools responding to pressures to raise test scores and prepare children for a competitive global economy, and, on the other hand, to create a joyful and stimulating learning environment. Choices get made by parents who both wish their children to receive recognition for outstanding achievements while also romping the playground without a care in the world.

Ultimately, choices about homework—how much should there be, how intensive the content—get made by teachers caught between conflicting influences. Teachers must respond to parents who covet for their child early admission to M.I.T. and to parents who prefer that their child spend her spare time exploring a range of cultural, recreational, leisure or athletic activities. Parents must deal with one teacher who assigns homework like it was an aspect of boot camp, and another who treats it as optional.

It's no wonder that there's confusion and misunderstanding.

Schools caught in this crossfire have a hard time behaving in a way that is visionary or wise. It's my sense that there will be no lasting peace in the homework wars until the interested parties—educators, parents, community leaders—sit down to talk it through. One suggestion for accomplishing this would be to hold community meetings on the subject.

A town meeting on homework need not be approached like a radio talk show, with each side shouting the supremacy of its position. Mediation is what's needed. Perhaps some hybrid policy can be conjured that can satisfy most, if not all, families without compromising core standards.

I don't have any easy answers. But with passions running high, I think it's time to get down to the hard business of working out a community consensus that can be reflected in sound homework guidelines.

For the good of the children.

WEBSITES

Homework Central *www. homeworkcentral.com*
Teaching Strategies *wwwteachingstrategies.com*
American Library Association *www.ala.org/parents/index.html.*

BOOKS

The End of Homework by Etta Karalovec and John Buell
Getting Our Kids Back on Track by Janine Bempechat

6

Learning How Your Child Learns

It comes as no surprise to you that your child is special. And you certainly believe that this uniqueness extends far beyond the obvious physical features—her hair, her smile, her distinctive way of curling into a chair while reading.

Your child notices things you might not notice (while remaining oblivious to things you consider fascinating), recoils in alarm from harmless experiences while plunging headlong into others more perilous, perks up at a kitchen table discussion of one topic while dazedly tuning out during the discussion of another, prefers audiotapes to books (or vice versa), and books to movies.

The list of your child's unique features goes on and on. But what does that mean for her schooling? What *should* it mean?

When I was in school, *differences* were synonymous with *difficulties*. The more you did things differently, the more difficulty you were likely to encounter. This environment tended to be particularly unsympathetic to students who had trouble responding to standard, unwavering teaching practices. The successful child was the one who got with the program, and stayed with it.

To some extent, that has not changed and maybe that's okay. Public schools are where society introduces its children to common values and shared knowledge. A certain uniformity needs to be part and parcel of the mission of schools.

Yet teachers are amply aware that there are multiple pathways leading to those uniform curriculum objectives, and that the quickest and best route for one child might not be so for another. Thus, the concept of "learning styles" has entered the vocabulary fairly recently.

In this chapter, I will explore what we know about learning styles, how recent developments in neuroscience contribute to our understanding of children's brains and how they learn, and how teachers and schools are clamoring to adjust to this rapidly evolving area.

Some of this field can be considered debatable (and is being debated as you read this) and some of it is widely accepted.

That the concept echoes the experiences and observations of good teachers gives it an added legitimacy. Long before there was neuroscienctific vocabulary for it, good teachers made a practice of shaping instruction to the learning strengths of individual students.

Schools, of course, vary in their ability to fully put into practice what we've recently learned about how children learn. Regardless, any step that takes you, or the teacher, or your child, toward a larger awareness of how your child learns is bound to pay dividends throughout his school career.

Simply put, the more you know about how your child learns, and the more the teacher knows, the better your child will be able to learn.

(Note: In trying to discern your child's learning style, you may find yourself wondering about your own. Chances are, the school you attended paid scant attention to this area. Focusing on your child's learning style can provide an introduction to another intriguing project: learning how *you* learn!)

What Is a "Learning Difference" and Why Does It Matter?

Teachers have long known that children learn in different ways, and do so at widely varying rates. "Learning differences," as I use the term here, refers to the distinctive ways in which each child, based on their unique makeup, best receives and processes information.

There are competing theories of how and why this happens, and each has its own nomenclatures and system of categorization. Much of the ground-breaking work in this field was done by Dr. Howard Gardner of Harvard University, author of *Frames of Mind: The Theory of Multiple Intelligences,* and Professor Rita Dunn of St. John's University, co-author of *Teaching Students Through Their Individual Learning Styles.* There are many other names associated with both recent and ongoing development of these ideas, as well as with the rapidly evolving neuroscience research that informs them.

None of these theories is indisputably the right one, yet most share a core understanding that forms the basis for much of what I will discuss.

The most fundamental contention of the notion of *learning differences* is that children (actually, all people) have strengths and weaknesses when it comes to learning. These can be identified according to what type of learner the child is, and knowing this *may* facilitate aspects of the child's education.

The broadest categories of learning differences are:

- *Auditory.* Some children learn best by listening.
- *Visual.* Some children learn best by reading and seeing graphic displays.
- *Kinesthetic.* Some children learn best by moving and actively doing.
- *Tactile.* Some children learn by touching and physical manipulation.

Additionally, Gardner posits several forms of "intelligence":

1. *Logical/mathematical.* Inclined toward math, science, problem-solving
2. *Verbal/linguistic.* Inclined toward words and their meaning, explaining, listening
3. *Bodily kinesthetic.* Jumps right in, inclined toward movement, sports
4. *Visual/spatial.* Prefers building, painting, graphic displays

5. *Musical*
6. *Interpersonal.* Empathizes with others, and needs to relate to them
7. *Intrapersonal.* Self-awareness, the ability to be reflective

Reviewing this list, it is obvious that the first two (logic-mathematical and verbal-linguistic) types of intelligence are the ones primarily emphasized in schools. Children strong in these areas may have an easier time being successful students. Children who are principally intelligent in the other ways may find school more challenging.

There are many schools of thought about the nature and method of *learning differences,* and they fall under a variety of labels and orientations (environmental, brain-based, hemispherity-icy). I am not in a position to determine which is most accurate or most useful. I recognize that in the profusion of theories there are bound to be some that are more speculative and untested. Many contain something of value. None of them, as far as I know, provides all the answers.

The ultimate message of work in this area is the increasingly widespread recognition that *all children have strengths,* and their education will be expedited and enhanced by knowing what those strengths are and how to adjust to them.

Furthermore, should your child encounter academic difficulty or be in need of special services, specific information about her learning style may prove valuable in developing IEPs (Individualized Education Plans—see Chapter 10) and other remedies. Teachers, tutors, and resource staff may find this information useful in working with your child.

Discovering How Your Child Learns

You are in the best position to know how your child learns. You have spent the most time by her side and have by far the largest folio of observations and experiences to call upon. You know what books she's liked and disliked, what her attention span is for various activities from audiotapes to legos. You know what kind of listener she is, and how that might change depending on circumstances. You know if she has an inclination toward mechanical objects or painting or music or athletics.

What you probably don't have is a method for focusing this intimate and multilayered knowledge in a way that can contribute to your child's schooling.

Here are some types of learning difference observations worth noting about your child:

- Interest in hobbies, and how she goes about cultivating them
- Deciphers maps and logic puzzles
- How she fills her idle time (exclusive of TV and computer games)
- Capacity to follow written directions, like cooking recipes or toy assembly instructions
- Skill at imitating athletic task or other types of body movement
- Notices visual detail and remembers it
- Easily follows verbal instruction and is fascinated by conversation
- Likes to handle and manipulate objects while learning about them
- Needs to discuss what she's learned or it won't sink in
- Moves around while reading or doing schoolwork
- Asks lots of questions about almost every topic

Many of these observations are at your fingertips and you need only formalize them into a more categorical understanding. Identifying some or more of these traits will help you work with your child in effective ways, and will help the school do likewise.

As an exercise to assist your observations, you might try listing several things your child has learned successfully at home and analyze how this learning occurred. Similarly, a review of learning experiences that failed or were frustrating to your child can be helpful.

It should be noted that there are core skills which every student, regardless of distinctive learning strengths and weaknesses, needs to develop. These include mathematics, literacy, sticking to a task, adhering carefully to oral and written directions, and the ability to engage in conversation, to name a few. A child with demonstrable learning differences is by no means exempt from needing to develop and improve in these areas.

School remains, foremost, our way of teaching the methods and values and behavior which our society believes will benefit your child. The point of tuning in to learning differences is to help your child do just that.

How This Information Can Help

If you have drawn some conclusions about how your child learns and what she most responds to (as distinct from other personality details, like shyness) you should convey this information to the teacher.

A critical part of teaching is understanding how individual children learn. Even teachers who are quite astute in this regard can be hampered by the demands of multiple responsibilities. This is where you can help.

Pam Broome, an educational consultant in Fairfax County, Virginia, suggests a note to the teacher at the start of the school year. This note might begin, "I thought you'd like to know a little bit about my child . . ."

Some teachers ask parents to fill out an extended questionnaire about their child, and many of the questions seek to illuminate concerns about learning differences. Without always designating it by name, many teachers frequently strive to discover the learning differences of their students.

For example, prior to the start of the school year, Middle School of the Kennebunks in Maine has parents evaluate the student on all of the seven formal Multiple Intelligence capacities. Prior to the seventh grade, the student is asked to evaluate himself. The instructional sheet says, "Our school is designed to give each of you the "gift of possibilities as you develop your intelligences. Look at each of the areas of multiple intelligences in this folder. List experiences that you have had either at school, at home, or in the community that would be indications of strengths in any of these areas."

Teachers, particularly those inclined toward an awareness of learning differences, will usually keep an keep an eye out for how and in what specific context your child:

- Shows enthusiasm for a subject or lesson
- Tunes out when others are fascinated
- Absorbs complex material
- Remembers minor details
- Participates eagerly in class discussion
- Seems lost despite making a strong effort

How a teacher approaches the broad notion of learning differences varies widely. For some it is an afterthought. Others employ a formal evaluation. Even where that is done, it is often just a piece of an overall assessment rather than a separate and dedicated effort.

I mention this because recognizing *learning differences,* for the most part, occupies a sort of netherworld in the swirling daily duties of a classroom teacher: It's a tool that teachers probably appreciate but may lack the time, resources, or training to completely utilize.

. . . .

Murfreesboro, Tennessee: Do-ers, Visual Learners and the Ear Group

Eliza struggled from the very start of school, and yet she loved it. She wanted to do well. She valued reading and learning. But like an awkward dancer placed in a ballet class, the fundamentals seemed to elude her.

"She just couldn't understand the concepts,'" reports her mother. "She worked hard and still she'd get bad grades."

In kindergarten and first grade, Eliza was extremely slow to read. The teachers were baffled. Eliza seemed bright enough to them, but the lessons that seemed effective with other children produced scant progress with her.

Her mother had her tested, but no glaring disability was discovered. Her mother enlisted her in a private tutoring program that came highly recommended. Other children who'd been lagging behind had made great strides with these tutors. Sadly, it did Eliza no good.

In second grade, Eliza fell further behind. Although she remained determined with an upbeat attitude about school, her mother wondered how long that would keep up.

Then in third grade she was assigned to the classroom of Cindy Jones, a teacher who's made a specialty of adapting to the different learning styles of her students.

Like many teachers, Jones had long been frustrated by the predicament of children she had tried desperately to help but simply could not find the way to do it. Most perplexing of all were the children outside the formal scope of learning disabilities who for some imprecise reason found it extremely difficult to learn.

Years ago, there'd been a boy thought to have suffered mild brain damage from an early childhood neardrowning. To Cindy, the boy had a brightness and intelligence that never quite showed up in the formal modes of school learning. Sadly, she never was able to get through to him.

Soon thereafter, there'd been a girl who was utterly unexceptional in every way. Except occasionally the girl would emerge out of nowhere with an astonishingly insightful and complex answer in class. Since this showed up so rarely and was far outweighed by the overwhelming mediocrity of the girl's work, Cindy, though baffled, was stymied. Several years later, the news got back to Cindy that the girl had moved on to middle school where she'd finally been formally tested. The girl was determined to have a genius level I.Q., coupled with extreme learning disabilities in language processing. Cindy felt horrible.

Shortly after these incidents, Cindy attended a workshop offered by the Tennessee Education Association on ways to diagnose and adapt instruction to the learning differences of children.

"It was," says Cindy, "like water to a person dying of thirst in the desert." The idea that the multidimensionality of children, a fact which teachers tend to believe is indisputable, can be an asset and not an impediment opened up exciting new vistas of opportunity for her.

Cindy began reading books, attending more workshops, studying brain physiology ("I knew nothing about how the brain works and here I'm supposed to be a teacher," she remarks self-deprecatingly.), eventually going on to earn a masters degree in developmental psychology.

But it was in the classroom where Cindy's newly acquired insights would be tested. Could she now help children in ways that she'd previously been unable to do?

When Eliza began third grade with Cindy Jones, she realized very soon that this year would be different. Perhaps haunted by past failures and oversights, Cindy vigorously tries to find within each child (especially those who are struggling) the ways that they are individually best able to learn. She does this is by "profiling" each student according to a range of traits.

For doing this, Cindy employs the Reading Styles Inventory method developed by Marie Carbo (several such diagnostic measures are available to teachers; there's wide disagreement among educators about which, if any, work best). Cindy develops a profile of each student that suggests to her whether a student, for example, has strong analytic tendencies, lacks tactile strengths but has excellent auditory perception, is not peer-motivated but is self-motivated, and needs relative quiet while working. Knowing these qualities, Cindy contends, allows her to teach with heightened focus on the needs of individual students.

For Eliza, this meant emphasizing the tactile and audio components of learning, even when the subject is reading. Cindy employs a range of colorful (literally) ways to help children with reading.

"Visual learners, over here," she announces at the start of the class's regularly scheduled reading session. All children have been reading the story, "Sarah, Plain and Tall" but the reading session will be broken into groups, which Cindy has organized into three categories: visual; auditory (or "ear group," as it's known); and tactile "do-ers."

Eliza is assigned to the do-ers or kinesthetic group. As they discuss "Sarah Plain and Tall," a conch shell is passed around. Children discuss the symbolic role played by such a shell in the story (it's the valued possession of an eastern-born woman married to a Midwestern man who's never been to the sea). Next, Cindy passes to each child a paper on which she has written, unsequentially, a list of plot elements. Students are asked to cut the paper along dotted lines and arrange the plot elements chronologically.

Cindy acknowledges that the categories are imprecise, and that some students might just as easily fit in one group as another. "The key," she explains, "is to give them some emphasis they can use."

Eliza and her mother report it's working. Exactly how, they are not sure. Perhaps it's using shaving cream to write out difficult words at home. Or memorizing the rules for sentence construction by means of a catchy jingle. Or being encouraged to use personalized hand gestures when struggling to sound out words.

Sure, Eliza still flounders. Academic prizes may still be out of reach. But suddenly she has a confidence that learning is within her grasp.

"Ms. Jones makes me feel like I can do it," Eliza enthuses.

. . . .

Will New Understandings from the World of Brain Research Impact My Child's Education?

"Neuroscience used to look at damaged or disordered brains," contends David Sousa, a consultant to school districts exploring innovative approaches to teaching and learning. "Now we study 'normal' brains."

In recent years, there have been a number of findings from the world of neuroscience with potentially significant implications for schools. Brain-based learning (as it is sometimes called by theorists and enthusiasts) offers intriguing and potentially valuable insights that currently enjoy only sporadic application in the real world of classrooms.

Findings in neuroscience promise to have some influence in such important areas related to education as:

Attention. We have learned that contrast, novelty, and a change in environment stimulate students' attention. Where these qualities are absent, students are bored and discipline is most likely to be a problem.

Memory. The brain learns best when presented with novel and finite chunks of information that can be meaningfully related to what it already knows. Long stretches of factual presentation poorly matched to student interest are most difficult to recall.

Positive emotional connections support memory and vice versa. Students are not likely to remember information presented in a context of shame, embarrassment or anger.

Timing. There are developmental periods—so-called *windows of opportunity*—when a child's brain optimally learns. This tends to be between the ages of two and eleven. The learning of certain challenging skills, like music and foreign languages, should probably be launched during these ages.

Remember, this is the optimal time for learning certain skills but it does not mean these skills cannot be learned later. It might just require more effort.

Interactivity. The brain learns best when the senses are stimulated. This can occur when students occupy a dynamic and colorful room, are encouraged to periodically move about, interact with the teachers and peers, and are engaged in tasks that go beyond passive listening to involve stimulating mental and physical activity.

As with learning differences, the developments in neuroscience do not, on the face of it, present us with insights that are altogether new or radical. At most, thus far, this research validates what good teachers have long believed to be true and may serve to convince more teachers, and schools, and parents to consider incorporating these ideas into their instruction.

What Next (Now That More Is Known About Your Child's Learning Differences)?

As I've discussed elsewhere in this book, teachers have an array of options for accommodating the differentiated needs of students. Most of these fall under the general category of modifications. Some of these can be relatively easy to manage, like:

- Moving your child's desk closer to the front
- Permitting her to move about and interact with peers when appropriate
- Allowing additional time for tests and other projects
- Using teaching materials that involve multiple senses

Meeting the diverse learning needs of individual students varies from teacher to teacher. Some improvise on the spot while others might be able to set aside time during a given lesson.

You may be curious how and to what extent the teacher pays attention to learning differences in your child. Teachers are approachable. You can ask:

- What effort do you make to discern a child's learning style?
- Have you noticed anything about my child that you could classify as a learning difference?
- Are there specific ways this information about my child's learning style can help with schoolwork?
- Is my child aware that she has a certain learning difference?
- Are there other children in the class with differences similar to my child? If so, are there adaptations you make?
- Are there things I can do at home to help my child better utilize her learning style?

Realistically, a classroom teacher with twenty or more students can only do so much in this regard. Tailoring instruction to many different students is a daunting job. Consequently, modifications that require more effort and time on the part of the teacher (like adapting entire lessons to suit different learning styles) may not fit so neatly into the constraints of the class.

If you feel more can be done to take advantage of your child's learning differences, it might be a good idea to meet with the teacher to try and develop some realistic options. Maybe there are steps you can take at home. Perhaps you can help with supplemental tools (audio tapes, museum visits) to better serve your child's specific learning differences. It's important to acknowledge to the teacher that you realize this is not an easy assignment.

The Big Picture

The emerging focus on learning differences sometimes does little more than provide a name and explanation for practices that good teachers have employed for generations. For that reason I hesitate to stress their importance.

Additionally, I am keenly aware that many classrooms in many schools are a long, long way from being anywhere close to implementing a policy of fully diagnosing and then adapting to the varied learning styles of their students. I am always reluctant to see parents get excited about classroom practices that even the best of schools can only sporadically deliver. And individualized accommodation to this most individualized of education concepts is certainly outside the routine capability of many schools.

That said, I believe there is merit to cultivating a learning difference sensibility in schools even if we recognize that it may never become the focal point of their existence.

Why?

Because recognizing learning styles reinforces and legitimizes an educational value that sometimes gets lost in the shuffle. It's a value that needs to be honored and preserved—especially as the pressure mounts for schools to produce a form of learning that is standardized and uniformly measurable. The value I speak of is one every parent holds dear: Each child is special and unique.

Legislators and commentators can resort to statistical analysis, norm-referenced district-by-district overviews and other modes of broad-scale assessment. But the real life of a school is ultimately judged, at least in the minds of parents and anybody else who truly cares, one child at a time. Doing our utmost to develop the innate talents of every child, helping them to "be all they can be" is what we strive for.

Of course, the public demands that it all to add up to a concrete result. With the pressure being applied to schools today, any new method or approach must convincingly demonstrate that it can pay off in terms of student achievement. That is as it should be. Ideally there ought to be no conflict between the broad goals of the school system and your specific objectives as a parent.

I'm enough of a traditionalist in my own beliefs about education to realize learning difference theory may rub some people the wrong way. They will see it as a deviation from the rigorous mission of getting students to buckle down and do work that is sometimes unpleasant. They might view it as yet another indulgence of a generation of students who are too pampered already.

I don't see it that way. Rather, I view learning difference methods as a promising way of helping children. It may be that we never arrive at a comprehensive, fully implemented, school-wide means of bolstering each child's unique ability to learn. But every concrete step we take in that direction is a step well worth the effort.

BOOKS

Frames of Mind: The Theory of Multiple Intelligences
by Howard Gardner
*Bringing Out the Giftedness in Your Child: Nurturing Every
Child's Unique Strengths, Talents, and Potential*
by Rita and Kenneth Dunn
*Educational Care: A System for Understanding and Helping Children
With Learning Problems at Home and in School* by Mel Levine
A Mind at a Time by Mel Levine
Teaching With the Brain in Mind by Eric Jensen

7

Standardized Tests

Standardized testing. Today, no other aspect of education gets as much attention. It's virtually impossible to have a child in public school and not find yourself sooner or later embroiled in discussions about standardized tests.

It's easy to become perplexed by much of this. Somehow, your child's school does not strike you as the proper place for a controversy of this magnitude. The classroom usually seems more like a sanctuary than a pressure cooker, as teachers and students (your child among them) earnestly go about their traditional pursuits.

But outside the school walls, there's a growing swarm of controversy.

On the surface, it might strike you as a massive disconnect, this yawning gap between the busy fever of daily life inside the school and the weighty, abstract arguments swirling outside. So different are these twin spheres, that they hardly seem to occupy the same world.

But they do. And that may be the reason for your discomfort. For standardized tests are where the political arena strides through the schoolhouse door and announces, "I'm here!"

At least for the foreseeable future, these tests will be a prominent feature of the public school experience. How prominent and toward what end are questions that remain to be answered.

An important distinction to keep in mind: *standards* and *testing* are not the same. Although the two are frequently intertwined by politicians and pundits, your thoughts about the former should be kept separate from your beliefs about the latter.

Standards is the concept that schools must embrace a challenging and well-defined set of academic objectives. To achieve these standards, teaching and curriculum should be rigorously aligned.

I fervently believe that higher standards and the allocation of resources for achieving them are vital to school improvement.

Standardized testing is the tool by which state and national (and sometimes regional or local) agencies measure student performance.

High Stakes Testing is where a student's score (or a school's) is deemed instrumental to certain outcomes, such as moving to the next grade level or graduating. Not incidentally, these tests carry high stakes for teachers and administrators (in terms of employment and salary) as well as for schools and school districts.

I have been passionately engaged in these issues for many years. I strongly support and vigorously advocate high standards. My views on testing, however, are far more complicated.

I wonder if there isn't a better way.

What Are Standardized Tests?

The standardized tests that are generating so much controversy are exams in which all the items on the test, the way the test is organized, the time allotted for the test, and the way in which the test is scored is, for the most part, the same for all those taking it. A standardized test is the same for all students of a certain age or grade level, regardless of school, within the established boundaries, which are usually defined by state, region, or nationally. In this way, the test provides a common measure of students' performance.

Standardized tests vary in quality and can consist of multiple choice, fill-in-the-blank, short answer and/or essay questions. These tests are to be distinguished from:

- Classroom tests, which are largely developed by teachers in order to provide a detailed view of what students know

- Diagnostic tests, which are "standardized" but are given on an individual basis, usually as an attempt to ascertain a student's strengths and weaknesses
- Intelligence (I.Q.) tests, which test for aptitude rather than achievement

Some Testing Terminologies You Should Be Familiar With

Norm-referenced tests are designed to measure how your child ranks compared to a national norm group or sample of students. This is done by placing students within a distribution of scores from low to high. Results usually fall along a distribution commonly known as the "bell curve." The average is fiftieth percentile. Half the children will be above that average and half below in the norm group. Questions are usually multiple choice and some questions are designed to be virtually impossible for a child to get correct, in order to "spread" students out along the distribution.

Criterion-referenced tests are designed to measure how your child ranks in comparison to a set of standards (academic in content) about what she should know and be able to do at that grade level. In theory, every child should be able to get all the answers correct on a criterion-referenced test provided she has been given good instruction and no disabilities exist. Scores are reported in regard to the amount of the content your child gets correct and not in comparison to other children. Criterion-referenced tests are usually developed by states with the help of outside consultants to match a state's content standards. Criterion-referenced tests are usually considered standardized. Some states are experimenting with performance assessment and portfolios (accumulation of a student's work) as ways to assess learning achievement.

High stakes testing is where a student's score (or a school's) is crucial to certain outcomes, such as moving to the next grade level or graduating. Similarly, tests can have high stakes for teachers (in terms of employment and salary) as well as administrators and schools.

Performance assessments are ways to measure student

achievement using essays, oral presentation, projects, and detailed explanations rather than relying on multiple-choice or short-answer tests.

Portfolio assessments measure a student's achievement based on a collection of his work, including papers, drawings, teacher evaluations, as well as test scores.

What Standardized Tests Will My Child Be Given and What Will They Be Like?

Many states test in grades four, eight and eleven. These commonly are criterion-referenced tests which may take from one hour per subject in four subject areas, depending upon grade level, to a series of partial days lasting up to two weeks.

Many states and districts also use a "norm-referenced" test, particularly for reading and mathematics. Each of these tests, which are often given in alternate grade levels (say, three, five, seven) lasts approximately one hour per subject area. Both tests measure achievement. Norm-referenced tests are usually purchased off-the-shelf.

According to recent research, fifteen states test every child at every grade level in reading and math from grades three to eight.

These criterion-referenced exams are created by individual state departments of education or related agencies, often with the assistance of professional testing services with considerable experience in this field. These tests go by different names in different places. Virginia's Standards of Learning (SOL) exam. The Texas Assessment of Academic Skills (TAAS). The Massachusetts Comprehensive Assessment System (MCAS).

Test week (or weeks) is a significant event around most public schools. The test usually occurs in the spring, and stretches across three to five days, usually not more than two to three hours per day.

Test week can sometimes be a tense and cranky time. Schools

often attempt to lighten the mood by granting more extended recess time or giving the afternoons over to less strenuous activities.

Children will usually be briefed about what to expect, at least concerning the demands of sitting and concentrating for extended periods of time. They will be told how much time they have to take the test, and what types of breaks and interruptions are permissible. More and more (see below), teachers familiarize children with a range of test-taking techniques.

The amount of pressure your child will feel around these tests depends on many variables, including how much the test matters to the school, the principal, and the teacher.

Most schools recognize that ratcheting up the intensity can have a boomerang effect on the performance of children. Schools that are heavily invested in test results, as more and more are compelled to be, usually try to prepare their students piecemeal over time to avoid a pressure-packed Superbowl atmosphere.

Schools must straddle an awkward position with regard to these tests, caught between an obligation to make sure their students do as well as possible and having significant misgivings about the merit of fully pursuing such a goal. Thus, it is easy for schools to fall into the trap of communicating mixed messages.

What Are the Goals of the Tests?

The *stated goals* of state-mandated standardized tests are usually:

- To assure the public that all students possess basic skills and that educational standards are taken seriously by the schools
- To inform communities about how their schools are doing
- To provide a means of measuring the quality of teaching
- To diagnose weaknesses and identify areas of need
- To determine necessary school reforms

A well constructed test properly aligned to curriculum can, to a degree, accomplish the above goals. In theory, such a test would enable teachers and parents to learn more about the strengths and deficiencies of the student and allow cities and towns to learn more about the accomplishments and failings of individual schools.

Flawed tests that are perceived to have an effectiveness and utility that, in fact, they do not have can, however, damage all these objectives.

What Does Your Child Think About the Test and Its Importance?

Your child should have a clear understanding of why the test is being given and what importance the school—and you—place on it. In that regard, you should know:

- What have the teacher and the school told your child about the test? How do they characterize it? What qualities do they say are being tested?
- To what extent your child believes that her test score reveals significant information about her achievement or learning
- If your child believes the test reveals significant information about the achievement or learning of her teacher
- If your child believes the test covers material she has been taught and should have learned

When Are the Test Results Received and How Are They Used?

Most states do not issue their results until the fall of the school year following the one in which the test is taken.

The results are issued on a statewide, district-wide, school-wide, and individual basis. All but the individual scores and the class scores will be available to the public.

Results may be used by state administrators in evaluating the performance of school districts.

Results may be used by school districts in evaluating the performance of principals.

Results may be used by principals in evaluating the effectiveness of teachers.

Clearly, results usually arrive too late to be of any benefit to your child for the class in which the test was taken.

What do Test Results Reveal About Your Child and the School?

You want your child to do well because, even if you believe the test to be seriously flawed, you know it reveals *something* about her. But what does it reveal?

A superior score probably means that your child knows the basic subject matter and possesses sound fundamental test-taking skills. Whether it means much beyond this depends very much on the overall integrity of the test.

Similarly, a weak score probably means that your child has less than a firm command of the subject matter and may certainly have weaknesses when it comes to the mechanics of test-taking.

School districts and departments of education should make every effort to help parents interpret test scores.

If you are not sure what a test score means, ask the school district for help. No test score should be interpreted without other accompanying information about your child, such as other test scores or written reports covering multiple areas of learning. Definitions of terms like "passing" and "proficient" should be clear according to specific standards.

The most useful standardized tests are those that can diagnose the strengths and weaknesses of current teaching and learning, and do so in ways that inform future teaching and learning. Standardized norm-referenced tests are often weak in providing the detailed information that a teacher needs to improve instruction for each child. This is why there has been a movement toward criterion-referenced tests.

Ultimately, in order to be effective, information from standardized tests must be presented in ways that students, teachers, and parents can learn from.

Because each state creates its own tests and its own standards, huge differences in performance standards exist. This can make it very hard to know how your school compares. It is the reason that norm-referenced tests, which compare each child to a national sample, are sometimes preferred.

Nonetheless, poor test results for a school or a district ought to concern any parents or guardian with children attending that school.

Standardized tests, both norm- and criterion-referenced, rarely provide teachers with information about students that they did not already possess. With few exceptions, the children who score well are already known by their teachers to have those capabilities. Similarly, children who flounder on the tests have for the most part already been identified by teachers as lagging behind their classmates.

Teachers should know how your child has done on homework, projects, quizzes and tests and portfolios gathered over time. Indeed, it would be a surprise if the standardized test told the teacher much about your child that she did not already know. If your child's test results do not match what you or the teacher knows about your child, then the fault probably lies either with the test itself, your child's motivation to take the test, or the alignment of the test to what is being taught.

To the extent that schools and families would like more detailed insights into the strengths and weaknesses of students in an array of academic skills, the standardized tests are unlikely to provide this.

Franklin County, Virginia: Standards of Learning

On the face of it, Gloria Anderson would seem to be a poster spokesperson for the movement toward standardized testing.

A former Virginia Teacher of the Year and beloved first-grade teacher with a specialty in gifted and talented children, Anderson left full-time teaching after thirty-five years in order to take a position with her home district, Franklin County, helping other teachers adapt to the mounting pressures of the state's notoriously difficult Standards of Learning (SOL) exams, which are currently given in grades three, five, eight, and high school.

This career switch seemed especially surprising in light of an op-ed article Gloria authored in September 1999, for a local newspaper. "Too many classrooms that were once enriched, productive environments for active learning and creative participation have now become stations for memorizing facts and names," she wrote.

What prompted such a dramatic turn-about?

Interestingly, Gloria does not view it that way. For her, the decision to take a leave from full-time teaching to work on behalf of a policy she had openly criticized was simply a continuation of her primary mission: helping children learn.

No, this did not mean that she has come to view the notoriously rigorous SOLs (97 percent of the state's schools posted failing marks the first year they were administered) as positive or benign. And it did not mean that she had retracted her prior reservations.

What it did mean was that Gloria believed there was an inevitability to the SOLs and their impact on schools, and the sooner teachers and families adjusted to it, the better it would be for the children.

"Since the SOLs aren't going anywhere," she explains, "we have to figure out ways to make them work better."

It hasn't been easy, but Gloria has taken up the challenge with all the vigor she applied in the classroom. Released from her full-time teaching duties, she immersed herself in a campaign, first to help rewrite curriculum for Franklin Country schools to reflect new state standards, and then to train teachers in ways to adjust.

The teachers, she realized, desperately needed help. They needed to know what of their old lesson plans were relevant to the new standards, and what no longer applied. All that required research and consultation, which Gloria diligently supplied. "Teachers," she points out, "don't have time to go flying into the library every time they need to check something out."

She taught classroom teachers what is in the state standards and how to match their instruction to what's contained on the test. She showed teachers tools for helping children learn in more concise and focused ways without, she hoped, completely sacrificing the creativity of teaching.

Gloria likes to think she has made a difference. But still, she is keenly aware of all that is being lost: classroom plays, field trips, and such "fun" supplements to the curriculum as music and art.

Do the children, she was asked, ever wonder why these aspects of their schooling have been dropped?

"They don't," Gloria answers with a sigh, " even have time to ask."

What Standardized Tests Do Not Say

To put the significance of these tests in context, it's important for parents to be aware of all that the tests cannot accomplish.

- Standardized norm-referenced tests are not diagnostic and the information they provide is of little diagnostic value.
- These tests rarely reveal information that will allow a teacher to understand your child's particular challenges or to better treat them.
- The tests, which *can* identify teachers whose students are not doing well, cannot help teachers figure out how to do a better job.
- There are emotional and health reasons why a competent student may perform poorly. (Kids, like adults, can have a bad day.)
- A student's skill at conceptual and critical thinking is rarely appraised in these tests.

One of the big problems in achieving greater parental understanding of the nature of standardized tests is the difficulty in learning very much about their substance. To prevent against cheating and to save the expense of continually revising the tests, most states do not permit public inspection of their contents. Except in a handful of states, the details of the test are known only to state education officials and participating reviewers. (Check with your Department of Education to see if you can see a copy of the exam.)

The problem this poses is obvious. If you cannot know in detail (and details are crucial in evaluating the merit of tests), then it is hard to precisely evaluate the test's merit. If you feel public oversight of standardized testing matters, then this situation must change.

Here are some common flaws found on standardized tests which should concern you:

- Questions that focus on trivia ("Who was the general of the Union Army at Gettysburg?") yet reveal little about the substance of a student's understanding
- A collection of questions about a topic that fails to properly emphasize for the student what is important to know, and what knowledge is being tested
- Questions that *are not* drawn from material that the teacher has taught, or was supposed to have taught

Standardized tests can be used as a broad indication of your child's achievement and school personnel can make adjustment at the program level. They are not useful in making individual decisions for children, particularly for high stakes such as graduation. Nor are they useful in evaluating overall school quality.

In the words of UCLA education professor, W. James Popham, "Trying to measure educational quality with a standardized achievement test is like trying to measure temperature with a spoon. It just doesn't work."

If These Tests are Flawed, Why Are They Used?

Standardized testing has clearly become the tool of choice for politicians intent on establishing "accountability" for public schools. "Accountability" in this context refers to the concept that in spending public funds schools must demonstrate, in quantifiable ways, that students are learning and that academic standards are being pursued.

It is thought, incorrectly in my view, that rigorous testing will provide a means of applying pressure to induce teachers and school administrators to upgrade their performance, and thus increase student achievement.

Clearly, the push for standardized testing reflects a concern about school quality. To the political establishment, this concern is intelligible only if it can be expressed in a concrete, statistical manner. The tests thus amount to an attempt to quantify how well, or poorly, schools and teachers are performing.

It is this urge to "quantify" the infinitely complex matter of teaching and learning where we run into big problems. The Nobel prize-winning physicist Albert Einstein reportedly kept a sign on his Princeton University office wall: "Not everything that counts can be counted, and not everything that can be counted counts."

So too with testing your child's education.

States are, however, clamoring to shore up some of the more obvious problems. States whose tests have been shown to contain demonstrable oversights and flaws are attempting to fix them, often by delaying high-stakes decisions based on the tests.

Throughout the country, curriculum is increasingly being aligned with state education standards. "Alignment" is the concept of coordinating and matching, starting with state education standards that find their expression in school curriculum, whose effectiveness can be measured by an "aligned" test.

If the test is a valid one, the alignment with instruction and curriculum is a positive development; if it is a flawed or improper test, then alignment hurts.

What's the Problem With Teaching to the Test?

When I was a teacher, I never really had to deal with standardized tests for which there were significant consequences. I don't know exactly how I would have handled it, for the tests create a quandary that can make teachers feel almost schizophrenic. On the one hand, if the test is being given and it counts, I would certainly want my students to do well. On the other hand, I would feel an intense obligation to my students to make sure the curriculum remained as broad and rich as possible.

As UCLA professor Popham points out, learning curriculum is different from learning "items." Items are defined as nuggets of information or material likely to find their way onto an exam.

As every teacher knows, the purpose of most tests is to provide a means for demonstrating—or discovering—the extent to which a student has mastered assigned material. Tests are devised to reveal a representative sample of what the student has learned.

Thus, in theory, if a student has mastered 65 percent of the lesson, the student should score something in the vicinity of a 65 (out of 100) on a valid, well-crafted test of the material.

What happens if the teacher, rather than focus on instructing the class in the wide range of a subject area (math, history, writing—you name it), chooses to narrow his efforts only to those sub-categories he suspects, based on tips, rumors, and past experience, will mostly likely be the basis for test questions?

Students will score higher. But have they learned proportionately more?

As Bill Harley, an entertainer popular at public schools, pointed out in a commentary broadcast nationally on NPR in May 2001, "Only yesterday a first-grade teacher told me she spent a whole week teaching kids how to fill in bubbles on standardized tests . . . You cannot measure the love for learning or a joy of knowledge or a passion for life. You cannot measure things with a standardized test, but you sure can kill them."

Also, there is a way that teaching to the test might, in a sense, diminish your child's learning. If high scores on a flawed test are the paramount goal, it can become "inefficient" for schools to teach material and methods not included on the tests.

In other words, if the test has shortcomings, if it is known to incompletely reflect the broad expanse of a subject area, then teaching to the test is a means of improving test scores and little else.

Quite simply, that is not good enough for our students.

Impact of the Test on Curriculum

A central argument behind standardized testing is to force underperforming schools (and teachers) to gear classroom instruction so students will learn the standard material stipulated by the state.

Proper alignment of the curriculum with state standards, so the theory goes, will create a seamless correspondence between what your child is taught in the classroom and what the state expects her to know. This is the idea at the heart of the so-called Standards Movement, which espouses the establishment of a core curriculum which all students need to learn.

I heartily endorse the move to raise standards, and have no quarrel with the policy of linking standards of curriculum to state tests. But what happens when the standards are vast and sprawling? What about those situations where the test does not align with standards?

This is where a standardized test can cause problems for teachers and students. The following are questions you might ask regarding the practice of teaching to the test:

- How does the content of the test reflect what your child has been learning in the classroom?
- What practices and activities have been changed or dropped to better prepare student for the state test?
- Are there curriculum areas not covered on the tests that will receive less attention because of the test?
- Are instructional areas, such as reading, being taught in more narrow and limited ways in order to mirror the test format, which features short paragraphs and multiple-choice questions?
- Has there been a reduced emphasis on more expansive types of assignments, like longer projects and reports, that do not conform to test format?
- Is there an increase in drill and memorization exercises

which can sometimes improve test scores without necessarily enhancing any deeper learning?

- What is the status of programs like music, art, and drama, which have little or no bearing on the standardized tests?
- How will the results of the test be used to benefit your child?
- Are there directives to teachers not to spend too much time prepping for the test?
- Are there curriculum areas not reflected in the test that the school declares to be valuable?

I suggest these questions not to scare you but to recommend parental surveillance of the way schools adapt to the pressures of standardized tests. Enhancing test-taking at the expense of student learning is, in my estimation, something to worry about.

What Types of Test Preparation Are Appropriate?

There are many useful ways for your child's teacher to prepare the class for a standardized test. Savvy principals and teachers, rather than sacrifice valuable curriculum, increasingly opt to spend some time teaching the mechanics of test-taking.

I see nothing wrong with this. Test-taking is a skill some students have always possessed, either by instinct or through special instruction. By actively teaching such skills, we effectively level the playing field—so long as the skills we teach are not merely tricks and ploys, and do not preoccupy the class.

What sort of test-prep techniques am I referring to?

- Familiarizing students with the format and time allotted for the test
- Helping students learn to budget their time during a test (i.e. learning to answer easier questions first, then returning for the more difficult ones)

- Instructing students on the careful reading of test passages and other resources included on the test
- Developing strategies for checking test answers
- Incorporating test-taking skills throughout the school year and employing them in regular instruction
- Involving students in discussion of the intent and purpose of the test
- Taking practice tests that include time limits and the format of the test

Frankly, I wish I had known some of these techniques during my grade school days.

Questioning Test Preparation Methods

There are forms of test preparation that I believe should be strongly questioned. These include:

- Teaching the exact items that will be on the test
- Excessive use of commercial test preparation materials
- Emphasis on test-taking tricks, like heeding the sequence of letters on multiple-choice answers
- School-wide pep rallies prior to the test
- Concentrating on material known to be included on the test while dropping significant areas of study

I recognize the inherent complications in passing judgment in an arena where the stakes are high and the ground rules are woefully ill-defined. Nonetheless, the goal of improved test scores can never justify questionable methods.

Relevant Facts

- Fewer than a dozen states report having high-stakes tests that are completely aligned with their standards.

- In a 2001 poll conducted for the American Association for School Administrators, about half of voters (48 percent) did not believe that standardized tests reflect what children know about a subject.

. . . .

Do All Students Have to Take the Test?

All students do have to take the state-mandated tests, unless explicitly exempted for a confirmed disability. Your school's resource counselor or special ed teacher can inform you if, and under what circumstances, your child's disability constitutes an exemption.

Also, if a student has documented disabilities, there may be accommodations that will permit your child to take the standardized tests.

In some schools, students and parents have refused to take the test out of protest. The consequences for such actions, if any, vary according to the situation and the state where it occurs.

What Is the Importance of these Tests?

To the state, the test results will serve as an evaluation of how the school is performing. The main distinction the state chooses to make is between schools performing adequately and those that are underperforming, in which case there may be sanctions.

To the school that is performing adequately, the test results have no immediate impact. To the school that is shown to be "failing," the possible consequences are profound, from the firing of the principal to revamping of curriculum. The state may also provide additional resources to help a school correct deficiencies revealed by the test.

To the principals, test results can profoundly impact their careers, including whether or not they are perceived to be successful. Some principals have contract extensions that are contingent on test score performance, or a bonus clause that relies on test score increases.

To *teachers*, standardized tests introduce a new and worrisome element to how they are evaluated. In some districts, teacher raises and hiring are influenced by test results in the teachers' classes.

To *the neighborhood or town*, test results are beginning to have an impact on real estate values. Realtors often furnish prospective home buyers with test score data about the neighborhood school.

To *your child*, the test's impact depends largely on how the school uses it, particularly if there are high-stakes consequences like promotion, retention, or eligibility for special opportunities like gifted and talented programs.

To *you*, the test and how it is dealt with may influence your perception of the school and, of course, cause you anxiety. I caution you to recognize that the tests are a piece of the whole picture, and no more than that.

The Big Picture

It's getting harder to remember that the original intention of the standards movement was to ensure that all students would have access to a more challenging curriculum.

Somehow that noble aspiration turned into the bureaucratically convoluted and politically driven demand for standardized testing.

Regrettably, high-stakes testing is having an effect that is almost the reverse of what was intended, narrowing the curriculum in ways not previously envisioned—as teachers, students, and administrators clamor to focus on the limited set of knowledge and skills they think will be covered on the tests.

Am I opposed to testing? To the contrary, I have been an outspoken advocate of rigorous assessment and accountability. I believe we should have an absolute standard for reaching achievement that every third grader should meet, and I would require testing to assess each student's progress.

Testing, of course, is nothing new. Students are and always have been routinely subjected to an array of tests, both standardized and teacher-generated. The issue is not: to test or not to test? The issue is how we focus our efforts, including testing, on helping students achieve.

An ideal testing program would provide information about student progress at the national, state, and local levels. It would be tied closely to curriculum and instruction and would offer teachers and students information about where instructional help is needed, what is being taught well and where improvement is needed.

The central aim of standards-based education is to strengthen student learning, not to rigidly regulate education in ways that, too often, thin the curriculum, reduce teaching to test preparation, and diminish student interest in schoolwork. Tests that do little but echo weaknesses in the system that we already know exist or, worse, skew classroom practices in ways that most educators find detrimental, can hardly claim to be for the good of the children.

I am worried that this campaign of high-stakes standardized testing is being launched without making a full and, yes, costly commitment to doing it the right way.

From all across the country, I receive the worrisome reports. Reports about teachers suddenly required to adopt a new curriculum without new textbooks or preparation. Reports about the adoption of new standards that read like a wish-list concocted by think tank theoreticians decades removed from a real classroom. Reports about test results stigmatizing underprivileged children for whom the bar has been raised without any corresponding effort to raise the level of instruction.

In many states, tests seem to be driving everything. They are driving curriculum and distorting the entire classroom experience of teachers and students. Materials we should be teaching are being systematically driven out by our growing obsession with testing. And the tests are driving many of our most skilled and creative teachers to look for other professions.

This is an issue that, depending on how it plays out, will radically affect the quality of our schools and the education your child receives. It is an issue on which politicians and business leaders and pundits have had their say while, oddly, the voices of parents and teachers have been largely absent.

That must change. Parents must become more informed about how standardized testing can help and how they can harm. Because most of what's being done—for good and ill—is being done in your name.

8

The Wired Classroom: Computers in Your Child's School

Back in your school days (and certainly mine), it was all pencils and paper and typewriters (optional) with correctable ribbons for special reports. The only deviation from traditional instruction was the periodic opportunity to view an educational movie or video. You could "interact" with it by applauding or yawning. Using calculators on school property was tantamount to cheating.

But you've come a long way since then. Despite your slow start, you are probably more "tech-savvy" than those cartoon grown-ups who must rely on their computer-whiz toddlers to guide them through every single click of the mouse.

After all, you've been exposed to various computers. You're familiar with certain types of software. The techie jargon of acronyms and abbreviations does not invariably leave you quizzically scratching your head.

In that respect, you are, at least partly, a citizen of the modern world.

And now you're sending your child to a school that boasts of being "wired" (or will soon be), has a part-time position for a technology education coordinator (or soon will), and claims a shimmering new computer laboratory that the kids all rave about.

So you think to yourself, great, my child is being prepared for the high tech future.

Then you pause a moment and wonder what that means. Are students learning to think for themselves or are computers making them mentally lazy? Are they acquiring skills that will boost their chances down the road? Are they learning new things, or is it just techno razzle-dazzle? You don't want to appear skeptical—in fact, you're not—but shouldn't this all be explained to you? Has anybody thought it through?

The wired classroom can be like a Rorschach test. What we read into its promise is likely to be a projection of the values we bring to the broader topic of what's best for our children.

Technology and learning is a relatively new area, and the focus of it has already undergone significant shifts. Only ten years ago, the emphasis was on developing "computer literacy" in students. Today, that is lower on the agenda.

As computers have evolved more user-friendly formats, changing so rapidly that none but the engineers could keep pace with it, many schools have come to recognize that the real objective is to use the technology as an educational tool—light sensors and temperature probes that allow students to do real science, graphing instruments to visually project mathematical relationships, conducting primary source research via the internet.

What intrigues me about the arrival on the scene of this spectacularly powerful tool is that it forces us to revisit basic questions: What is it we want our children to learn, and what methods do we prefer for getting there?

The discussion about computers and education is now taking place against the backdrop of a highly charged national push for a return to "basics" in education. Proponents argue that computers will revolutionize education for the better. Others say, "show us the proof."

The inarguable facts about computers and technology are:

1. They will play an increasing role in your child's school.
2. There will be tremendous variation in their usage, from teacher to teacher, subject to subject, and school to school.
3. The extent to which they will be integrated into classroom learning is very much an open question and subject to the influence of parents and community.

Computers will not solve the myriad problems of education, nor will they magically provide a pathway enabling us to neatly skirt around them. Computers hold great promise for enhancing learning, but they cannot settle for us long-standing debates about the nature and intent of a public school education.

What Is the Impact of Computers on Learning?

If computers worked like the proverbial charm, if you could plunk a child in front of a keyboard and monitor, install an appropriate software program, and after a designated time return to discover—presto!—a more educated child, this would be a less complicated discussion.

But for the most part, we still lack conclusive evidence about how, and if, computers and technology enhance learning. What we do know is:

- Computers can motivate students, particularly children who have been previously turned off from learning.
- They enable children, even those who have done poorly in school, to participate in learning, to effectively become a partner in many of the exercises.
- Test scores can be raised when the software specifically targets certain skills and the teacher knows how to use it.
- Computers and technology are most effective in supporting learning of complex tasks rather than basic skills.
- Children with disabilities can greatly benefit when academic work is augmented by appropriate software and hardware (assistive technology).
- Computers can shift some of the locus of power in the classroom from the teacher to the students.

Interestingly, much of what is discussed and hoped for regarding computers and learning is, at this point, conjecture.

When used well, computers certainly can have a role in helping kids learn a subject. If computers are not used well, if the software is uninspiring or the teacher uses it inappropriately, they don't help.

Things we do not know about technology and learning:

- Under what circumstances does the technology contribute to student understanding of subject matter
- How technology mediates learning
- How technology can be useful in providing teachers with meaningful assessment data
- How cultural background affects the influence of educational technology on a student
- Whether learning achieved by virtual means is the same as learning achieved in a hands-on fashion
- Whether the increase in motivation around computer learning sustains over time

What to Look for in Your School's Use of Computers

At the school open house or during a classroom visit, you are treated to a tour of the computer lab and given a demonstration of how computers are impacting teaching and learning. Monitors light up with glowing displays. Printers shoot out perfectly aligned paragraphs explaining color-coded bar graphs. You nod your head and smile.

I've been on many such tours and I am usually amply impressed. Then some time afterward, maybe on my ride home, I pause to ask myself: How do I know if these dazzling machines are being used wisely?

Some questions to ask:

- Does the school, and the district, have a technology plan?
- Does this plan contain instructional objectives, goals for integrating computers with content?

- Can students working at the computers explain what it is adding to their lesson, what the advantage is to using it?
- Do kids seem to be using the computers in a meaningful way (a subjective concept, to be sure, but one you'll want to be aware of)?
- Can the teacher explain how the technology enhances a lesson?
- Does the teacher receive ongoing help in how to integrate computers into their instruction?

The glitter may indeed indicate gold. But we owe it to our kids to sift through to the real thing.

What Is a Technology-Enhanced Classroom?

The term "technology enhanced" refers to a classroom where the curriculum, be it math, literature, science or ancient history, is augmented by *learning opportunities that derive specifically from technology*. If computers in the classroom are underutilized for this purpose, then all you have is a classroom containing fancy machines and software. It is not *enhanced*.

This is an important distinction to keep in mind. The central question is not how much technology exists in the classroom, and the relative sophistication of it, but rather: How is student learning improved by it?

The technology plan of most school districts—if they have one—will often contain language that stresses the use of computers "as a tool." The *integration of computers and curriculum*—using technology as a tool—has replaced the catch phrase of a few years back, "the wired classroom."

Why? Because experience has demonstrated that merely possessing the hardware and software does not automatically yield learning. The job is far more complicated than that.

Thus, a technology-enhanced school, in addition to computers and software, should have:

- Teachers comfortable with the technology and trained in how to use it
- Lesson plans that make use of the technology to invigorate and deepen learning, that reconceptualize those parts of the curriculum that can be taught a better way
- A tech support person available to handle problems
- A curriculum integration specialist to formulate ways to create lessons that involve the technology

Optimally, say experts, the ideally enhanced classroom would have:

- At least one computer for every three or four students with a reliable high-speed connection to the internet
- A scanner
- A digital camera, video camera, and video processing
- An electronic microscope and electronic probes
- Multimedia software
- Resource CDs on relevant subject areas
- A display or projection device
- Access to a computer lab for whole class instruction or projects

The classroom of the future already exists in piecemeal fashion. The hardware, the software, the digitalized augmentations, all can be found in our schools today. With very rare exceptions, however, these features have yet to be fully consolidated throughout a school or school system. And the most important component of all—the integration of computer technology as a tool that smoothly facilitates instruction and learning—is very much a work in progress.

It's important to note that the optimally equipped classroom of today will not necessarily be optimal tomorrow. It may still be useful, or it could be obsolete. For example, schools that bought stand-alone computers just as the internet became important found themselves in trouble.

Relevant Facts

- In 1990–91, schools and school districts spent $2.1 million for computers; in 1998–99, they spent $5.5 billion on computers.
- Less than 5 percent of schools' educational technology budget is spent on teacher training. (The U.S. Department of Education recommends that school districts spend 30 percent of their technology budget on teacher training.)
- Only 33 percent of K–12 teachers report feeling "prepared" or "very prepared" to integrate digital content into instruction.
- Very little research exists on the effectiveness of computers on learning in subjects other than math and science.

How Computers Are Used in Your Child's Classroom

Here are some questions you might want to have answered:

- What are the students actually doing with their time on the computer (and does it seem like learning)?
- When students are conducting internet research for school reports, are they analyzing their findings or merely performing cut-and-paste functions?
- In what way is the computer changing the teacher's role?
- When some students are working on the computer, what are other students doing?
- What steps are taken to prevent exploitation of students by businesses, web advertisers, or others?

- Is internet usage at school balanced with library usage, or is it replacing it?
- How does the teacher handle the plagiarism potential created by internet research?

Again, I do not suggest raising such questions because I am skeptical about the overall benefit of involving computers in school. But I do believe that schools should be accountable to parents for enlightened use of these tools.

Are There "Best Practices" Guidelines for Computers in the Classroom?

We are in a time of transition and there is wide variation in the use of computers in schools. Most schools do not have extensive guidelines for how teachers will use computers. That decision is mostly left to the teacher. Consequently, a child's exposure to computers in the classroom can be vastly different from teacher to teacher, class to class. Even within, say, the fourth-grade classes at the same school you can find significant differences in the technology they possess and the way it is used.

There are teachers who are comfortable with the technology and eager to find ways of incorporating it into their instruction. There are others who are wary and even skeptical of it. Most teachers find themselves gaining a piecemeal familiarity in fits and starts.

"I had to accept that I didn't know everything about it," said Mary Cate Riley, a teacher in Milton, Massachusetts, referring to her initial efforts to incorporate Hyperstudio software into the lessons of her fifth-grade classroom. "I had to let go of the control piece of it. Once I saw that the kids didn't really care if I knew every single thing about the program, I was more willing to attempt new things."

Teachers new to the profession are more likely to seek ways of integrating new technologies into their instruction, since it will be an important feature of their developing careers. More veteran teachers nearing the end of their career may not see the merit in devoting the extra hours it takes to familiarize themselves with what technology has to offer. Interestingly, the most avid adopters have been teachers with about ten years' teaching experience.

Many school districts do, however, have a technology plan that presents an overview of stated goals and possibly a timeline for the schools to achieve them. These goals can range from general aspirations (achieving computer literacy, preparing students to solve problems by using the latest technology) to specific targets, such as the following, proposed by the National Educational Technology Standards:

Prior to completion of grade two, students should be able to:

- Use input devices (mouse, keyboards)
- Use output devices (monitor, printer)
- Use a variety of media and technologies for independent learning
- Work cooperatively in using technologies
- Communicate about technologies using accurate terminologies
- Gather information and communicate with others using telecommunications, with support from teachers and student partners

By the end of grade five, students should be able to:

- Use telecommunications resources to engage in collaborative problem-solving tasks
- Use technology tools for individual and collaborative writing and publishing activities
- Use telecommunications and online resources to participate in collaborative problem-solving

By the end of grade eight, students should be able to:

- Collaborate with peers, experts, and others using telecommunications
- Design, develop, and present products using technology resources
- Demonstrate an understanding of concepts underlying hardware, software, and connectivity, and their practical applications to learning

There is general agreement, even among skeptics, that it is useful for your child to learn the following core functions:

- *Keyboarding:* how to type fluidly and use the keyboard controls
- *The four basic applications:* word processing, spread sheets, data base management, and graphics
- *Conducting research on the internet*

At minimum, these are thought to be skills that will carry over from new development to newer development, from upgrade to upgrade, fortifying a student for whatever new world of technology he or she eventually enters.

In other areas, such as multimedia presentations, for example, it is unclear what the usefulness will be a decade down the road as technology develops and changes. The use of graphics is a basic skill, although the particular kind of software will change. "The only things that goes stale faster than computers," warns William Rukeyser, former special assistant to the California State Superintendent for Public Instruction, "is milk."

The rapidity of change in computer technology presents a considerable challenge to public schools. The pace of developing and assessing innovative, educationally effective applications is much slower than the rate of technological advances.

In their effort to keep up, schools can sometimes make costly mistakes, buying ineffective or nonstandard hardware (as was done with Betamax video systems) or software. For all the eagerness on the part of schools to keep students current, there should be an equal caution about spending time and resources training students in technology functions that may could soon be outdated. "Sometimes schools cannot be on the leading edge," observes Gary Bloom, a former principal and currently associate director of the New Teacher Center at University of California-Santa Cruz. "The leading edge is moving too quickly."

I'm not sure what would be a perfect solution to this dilemma. I know that in the harsh reality of tough budget decisions, it will be crucial for schools to involve many stakeholders, not just the school board, in this discussion. It would be a shame for the true potential of the wired classroom to be undercut by a backlash resulting from unwise purchases.

Are There Practices to Avoid?

The following uses of computers and technology should be discouraged by the school, and should concern any parent:

- Reliance on computers for repetitive drill and practice exercises (These have been shown to actually diminish learning levels in some math tests.)
- Using computer time as a reward, particularly if the computer time is spent playing games or visiting recreational websites
- Having some students sit idly by as others use the machine
- Using computers as way to create "quiet time" in the class
- A stratified use of computers, with faster learners using computers for more advanced functions and slower learners using drill and practice programs

Jane M. Healy, a popular consultant on schools and technology, and author of *Failure to Connect: How Computers Af-*

fect Our Children's Minds—for Better or Worse, proposes several basic rules schools should follow, including:

- There should be clear supervision of student use of the internet and limited access to it.
- Computers must serve the curriculum, rather than the reverse.
- Classroom teachers, not administrators, should make the decisions about how to use the technology.
- The school must provide adequate technical support to the teachers.
- Schools should be mindful of the physical health impact of sustained computer usage, particularly to the eyes and neck.

If your child's school or classroom falls short in several or more of the above strictures, I suggest bringing your concerns to the teacher, the principal, and to other parents.

Can Computers Help to Improve Test Scores?

There is no doubt that computers will increasingly be enlisted in preparing children for standardized tests. What is not clear is whether this is an effective, or wise, method.

So-called "drill and practice" software has shown some effectiveness in improving scores on certain basic skills tests and, as mentioned earlier, has shown to have a negative impact on others.

What concerns many educators is that these drill and practice programs can amount to the least stimulating use of technology for children. As observers have pointed out, students are motivated to learn with computers as long as the work they do on them continues to be challenging. When computer tasks prove boring, kids eventually react the way they do when any form of instruction becomes boring: They tune out.

The more engaging computer applications appear to be the

ones that foster more complex, problem-solving types of thinking skills. These skills, however, are not usually central to the standardized, state-mandated exams.

As I mentioned at the start of this chapter, I am intrigued by how the wired classroom may force us to confront certain issues about education. The standards movement places this concern front and center.

Thus, we are at a crossroads. Computers appear most useful in facilitating forms of learning that are not closely aligned with the basic skills being emphasized by standardized testing.

Do we revert to using computers for the limited functions of boosting test scores, knowing we run the risk of tainting enthusiasm for the technology? Should we revise our notions of what constitutes "basic skills" in education, and accordingly adjust our testing criteria, in order to make best use of computers?

Or do we proceed as we are now doing, muddling through in improvised ways?

My own belief is that schools cannot be put in the position of adjusting to every exciting technological product that offers an educational application. The tail cannot be allowed to wag the dog. The best way for a school to make wise decisions about technology is to have a clear vision of teaching and learning. Developing and refining that vision is, or should be, an ongoing process. It's what makes education an exciting field.

Will (Should) Computers Alter the Way Classrooms Operate?

The guide on the side; not the sage on the stage is the phrase you hear for this new mode of teaching. The idea is that computer-enhanced, problem-based learning will enable students to play a more central role in their classroom.

Enthusiasts believe that computers can, in effect, free the teacher to play a new role. While still dispensing helpful information, the teacher will also facilitate the progress of ideas that kids are initiating and executing. The teacher will be there to correct misconceptions, but in the context of activities created by the students.

It is hoped that computers will free teachers and students from some relatively unimportant tasks so they can give more time to the important ones. For example, word processors take the drudgery out of physically cutting and pasting text. Graphing calculators let students plot changing parameters in an ellipse without having to redraw the figure again and again on graph paper.

As a veteran classroom teacher, and a bit of an old school one at that, I have mixed feelings about this. The best teachers, in my experience, have been adept at playing both the guide *and* the sage. Both roles are important. As Jane Healy puts it, "I believe in the guide leaning over the shoulder to answer a child's question."

....

South Burlington, Vermont: What's French for "Wired"?

For Barbara Gill, a South Burlington, Vermont, middle school teacher of French, her introduction into the world of technology and education began seven years ago with a workshop presentation on the critical role computers would play in the workplace of the future. The speaker, Willard Daggett, gave a vivid depiction of life in the twenty-first century coupled with a dire warning that Barbara would not soon forget.

"He (the speaker) said our kids needed to know about computers," Barbara recalls. "Otherwise, we would be letting them down."

Of course, it was not immediately apparent how a teacher of French would go about using her class to expand students' knowledge of computers. But in this effort, Barbara had two things going for her.

First, she is the sort of person who likes a challenge.

Second, South Burlington is a prime example of a community mobilizing itself fully toward technology-enhanced learning.

Located near a large IBM facility as well as the technology-rich University of Vermont, South Burlington had already begun serious exploration of how to bring computers into the schools. A technology committee comprised of teachers, school officials, and interested residents was vigorously planning how to increase the school district's technology program.

Funding was, as always, key. The technology committee put forward a bold proposal to raise, via taxes, an additional $365,000 per year for six years earmarked for technology in the schools. The tax increase passed.

According to Darlene Worth, director of curriculum for the school district, the schools did not have to sell the community on the idea. "They pushed us," says Worth. "The community really wanted to see their students educated for the modern world."

Barbara Gill quickly became an early adopter. Using her first classroom computer, she involved her students in email exchanges with students in France, writing to them, in French, about the holidays of Thanksgiving and Halloween.

"I got some flack from colleagues," Barbara recalls. "They thought I was just playing games with the kids."

Using computers to teach is, of course, not just playing games. But there is some of that spirit to the experience, and that is a key reason students are invigorated by technology in the classroom.

Barbara's efforts mushroomed into more complex and varied projects: "visiting" the websites of famous French landmarks like the Louvre and having the class write about them; using the program "Hyperstudio" to create multimedia descriptions of the changing seasons, illustrated by students and narrated by them using their best French accents.

Says Barbara, "What this (technology) does is take all the things I tried to make lively and real and authentic for my class, and makes it so much easier."

When machines occasionally crashed, as machines do, Barbara was prompted to join the technology committee. She argued for more tech support, and more teacher training if these new instruments were to be effectively used.

Teacher training is crucial if schools are to begin to realize technology's promise. With this in mind, the South Burlington technology committee decided to assign two knowledgeable and enthusiastic teachers to work full-time as trainers of other teachers.

You guessed it. Barbara Gill, once a French teacher with no particular predisposition toward computers, became an official "teacher leader" in technology.

She looks back with some amusement on the frustrations she had when she first started—the crashing machines, the discipline problems that occurred before she learned how to apportion computer time and create stimulating projects. "Now," she says happily, "I'm the poster child for using technology in teaching."

....

Can Being Wired at Home Allow You to Be a Better School Parent?

Some envision a classroom of tomorrow that uses computers in a way similar to what can be found today at many colleges: lesson plans available at websites, interactive messaging with faculty, remote access to class notes and assignments.

A fully wired—for the reasons stated above—classroom has the potential to enable parents to play a more informed role in their child's schooling. Parents with internet access could:

- Communicate with busy teachers without calling them at school (where they rarely have time to talk) or home
- Monitor expectations for homework assignments and long-term projects
- Review websites the teacher is recommending to students
- Assist the child in retrieving make-up work

We are not there yet. Schools remain concerned about fairness of access. Affluent students have greater computer opportunities at home. Districts scramble to create equity in computers-to-student ratios among the schools. Your school's ability to optimally integrate technology with learning may at least partly depend on giving all families the chance to fully participate.

The Impact of Future Developments on Learning

Experts who track the world of computers and learning point to several areas where better research and improved software could produce a profound impact on how schools incorporate technology:

- More research needs to be conducted into the effect of computers on children's attention span.
- The motivational aspects of computer learning need to be better understood.
- "Intelligent tutor" software needs to be developed that can analyze how a student arrives at right and wrong answers.

- Equipment must become easier for teachers to use, and less prone to glitches.

The Big Picture

We've come a long way from the era when learning the "hard way" was thought to be *the way* to build strong young minds. The hard way implied nose-to-the-grindstone exercises, not seeking short-cuts, not dressing up the onerous task of learning with fancy fun and games.

Thankfully, we left that model behind many years ago. Now with the advent of computer technology, we are rapidly approaching a new model for what and how we learn. We just don't know what that is yet.

The exciting aspect to this is that the forthcoming transition—and there is sure to be one—presents an opportunity to redefine what we mean by education, what we want from it. The word is out: Computers and technology, when it comes to education, are only as good as the learning and growth they facilitate.

Teachers, administrators, school boards, parents, and the surrounding business community will, in the coming years, be grappling to make sure that the new technologies, acquired at a steep cost, serve the educational objectives set forth.

If a fraction of the promise of computer-based learning proves true, we are entering a time when it will be more possible than ever to create classrooms that are adaptable to the learning differences of different children.

The changes brought about by integrating computers into classroom learning—whatever shape they take, and at whatever pace they proceed—will reopen long overdue discussions about what we want children to learn, and what kind of citizens we expect them to be. Educators, cognitive scientists, and technology developers will need to collaborate with each other and with parents on these issues.

The wired classroom is, to a certain degree, a fixture of future schooling. How we get there, and what values we choose to embrace along the way, are entirely up to us.

WEBSITES

George Lucas Educational Foundation *www.glef.org*.

Learning in the Real World *www.realworld.org*.

International Society for Technology in Education *www.iste.org*

National Center for Technology Planning *www.nctp.com*.

The Computer Learning Foundation *www.computerlearning.org*.

9

Making the Teacher
Conference Work for You

The time has arrived for your parent-teacher conference. You enter the classroom and there is an almost eerie emptiness, like a museum after hours. The walls are decorated with the multicolored offshoots of the students' efforts, artwork and maps and reproductions of historical events. The desks, tidied up, still display the pencils, text books, and folders the students busily use throughout the day.

But the students are gone.

Only the teacher is present. Along with you.

You know the time is short, no more than thirty minutes, and there is a lot of ground to cover. But now that you are here, you are not exactly certain what matter to take up first. Or second or third, come to think of it.

So you let the teacher take charge. Sitting awkwardly in the cramped chair usually occupied by your child, this seems like the right thing to do. If you have any questions, you can just raise your hand and wait until called upon.

No! You remind yourself that you are the parent, not the student. You are here for a serious purpose. But what is it? You want the teacher to like you, and by extension your child. Should you make jokes? Show off your intelligence, your sensitivity, your moral character?

The teacher lays before you your child's portfolio. It's crammed with papers and blue books and quiz results. Are you expected to sit there and read through it? That would consume the entire time. A fluttering of guilt surges through you. Should you already be familiar with all this stuff? Have you dropped the ball?

The teacher launches into some introductory comments. You listen, nodding, but you're not completely sure what she's referring to. She mentions a project you cannot remember, a curriculum goal you thought wasn't to be covered until next year, uses a baffling edu-speak term that leaves you feeling like the inattentive kid off daydreaming in the back of the class.

You glance at the clock. What? Half the time has already scooted by and you have no better idea of how your child is doing than if your child had briefed you herself.

On the other hand, you note that nothing horribly upsetting has come up. For that you are thankful. It's been like a visit to the dentist's office and you're happy to exit with no cavities discovered.

The parent-teacher conference occurs twice per year in most school districts, during the fall and spring. These conferences are an overlooked and often underappreciated feature of the public school experience, largely because expectations are often not very high. But I think this is a huge missed opportunity.

If approached the right way, this conference has the potential to set a positive tone and framework for your child's school year, and be crucial in developing a positive working relationship between you and the teacher.

Achieving an effective conference is trickier than you might think, however. Teachers, apprehensive of stepping on toes, can tend to pull punches in their comments or use terms and phrases that soften the impact of their remarks. Parents with a lackadaisical attitude tacitly encourage teachers to take it less seriously and parents with an axe to grind can put teachers on the defensive, chilling the discussion.

The sins of omission and commission are something I know firsthand, as both a parent and a teacher.

Teachers cannot help but pay special attention to children whose parents show a special and thoughtful concern. It's human nature to do so. So remember: Above all else, this conference is a chance to show your child's teacher that you deeply care about what happens in the classroom.

In my experience, that is worth a lot.

What Should You Expect?

Of the regularly scheduled teacher conferences, the one in the fall tends to be positive and upbeat, since relatively little has taken place up to this time and the teacher's knowledge of your child is still somewhat sketchy. There are, of course, numerous exceptions to this, particularly if your child is having difficulty adjusting.

For many parents, this conference is also the first chance to speak privately with the teacher. It is thus a "feeling out" of who this person is, and how best to relate to each other over the ensuing months.

By the time of the spring conference, your child's learning capabilities and social style will be well known to the teacher. This is your chance to get a full appraisal of how your child is doing and what, if anything, should be done to help her along.

The personal style teachers bring to these conferences ranges widely, depending on their personalities. Some are casual and solicitous. Others are more formal and by-the-book. Some have prepared a succinct presentation, after which you are free to ask questions. Others prefer give-and-take interaction right from the start.

Like any professional at an important meeting with someone (you) whom they do not know all that well, teachers are caught between the need to be outgoing and yet cautious. Some will take the lead. Others will follow yours. The thing to keep in mind is that there is no right or wrong approach. If a teacher's style might not be what you expected or are used to in vocational situations, remember that it is a style comfortable to the teacher.

Should You Prepare for the Conference?

Teachers can be most useful and responsive when parents are prepared to learn and contribute. An amiable but empty session does neither of you any good. It's important to give thought to your goals for each conference.

- What do you want to learn about your child's performance or development? (The more specific your questions, the better—generally speaking.)
- Do you have social as well as academic concerns?
- Are there issues—sloppiness, inattention—you want to focus on?
- Is there information about your child that the teacher could benefit by knowing (home problems can be mentioned without needing to go into specific detail)?

The teacher conference is a good excuse—not that you should need one—to sit down with your child and get, as best as possible, a briefing on how the school year is going. Before the conference, ask your child such questions as:

- Are you comfortable with the pace and style of the class?
- What subjects do you like or dislike?
- How do you feel about the teacher?
- Are there things you would like me to speak about to your teacher?
- Do you feel you are doing well?
- If not, what could help you do better?

Teachers appreciate parents who already have a sense of how their child is performing and have some idea of what is being studied. You are, of course, entitled to use the conference time to discover these things anew. But it might not be the most productive use of your time, or the teacher's.

Some general pointers:

- Be on time; if you are going to be delayed, call in advance.
- Get straight to the point if you have pressing concerns.

- If you have serious concerns, the conference will be more productive if the teacher is alerted at least a day ahead of time. (Similarly, if the teacher has serious issues to raise, you should be apprised in advance.)
- Be collaborative in your approach, not confrontational.
- Be mindful of how much time is allotted. Prioritize your agenda in case time runs out.
- Bring any papers or work sheets about which you have significant confusion.
- *Do not bring* younger siblings for whom you couldn't find a sitter.

I realize that you may be quite busy and that these conferences may catch you at a time that seems far from convenient. All I can say is try to leave your outside concerns at the classroom door.

What Is the Feel and Flavor of These Conferences?

Teachers see these sessions as a way to inform parents of key features of the child's school experience and to establish a positive working relationship.

The sort of parent a teacher most hopes to meet is one who is informed, concerned, and eager for collaboration. The fact that you and the teacher share an intense interest in your child's betterment should set the tone.

The sort of parent who makes a teacher most apprehensive is one who is uninformed and accusatory. You need not make it a goal to have the teacher "like" you, but you should be reluctant about being confrontational. There are better ways to get things done, and probably better forums for doing so.

Similarly, parents most appreciate teachers who are open and forthcoming, and are most discouraged by teachers who are defensive. Be mindful of the ways you can influence this dynamic.

Schools generally do not dictate the format. Individual teachers have their own way of conducting these sessions and should be happy to tell you what that is ahead of time. There are time constraints (usually half an hour) and a general obligation to cover significant school information. Regarding general guidelines, that's about it.

A stumbling block to an effective conference can be the use of code phrases or jargon that obscures what is *really* being said. For example, the following are terms with simple surface meanings that may actually mean more:

- "Emerging"—as in "your child's reading skills are emerging"—can be a way of saying developmentally sub-par.
- "Shy" and "well-behaved" can be terms for quiet and uninvolved.
- "Difficulty listening" can mean impulsive or disobedient

Many teachers use such coded and ambiguous terms out of faculty locker room habit, not to hedge or obfuscate. If their decoded meaning causes you concern, you should definitely seek further explanation.

You may be eager to hear good comments and wary of hearing anything negative; still, you should try to resist the tendency to accept a teacher's remarks without further explanation.

What Will the Teacher Do?

The teacher is likely to present you with some samples of your child's work (tests, papers, drawings) as illustration of both the classroom's methods and your child's performance.

My experience, having made hundreds of these presentations to parents, is that the material usually comes at them rather rapidly and their eyes tend to glaze over. My hunch is that this is due to the fact that most parents are very prone to view their children as performing within the general parameters of "okay," and almost anything the teacher says or shows them roughly confirms this.

Tacoma, Washington:
Creating a "Partnership Conference"

Schools, like most institutions, fall into habits that can be shaken when somebody who knows what she's talking about asks: Isn't there a better way? The standard parent-teacher conference may be one such habit, as Gayle Nakayama has demonstrated.

A reading specialist in the Tacoma, Washington, school district, Gayle knew that the regular conference was frequently underutilized, by parents and teachers. Too often, in her experience, this ripe opportunity was conducted as a polite obligation.

What, Gayle wondered, would happen if you took concrete measures to emphasize the possibilities? What if the school announced that this conference really mattered, and then provided families with the tools for seeing it through?

With a special grant from the NEA's Foundation for the Improvement of Education, Gayle set about the task of reconfiguring what she now was calling "the Partnership Conference."

The key elements she envisioned were:

- A questionnaire for the child's family, sent in advance of the conference
- Stated goals and objectives for the conference
- Full participation of the student, including attendance at the conference

"We felt that we had been starting out on the wrong foot with parents," explains Gayle. "We wanted to start out with more listening."

The Partnership Conference was first implemented four years ago on an experimental basis at Larchmont Elementary, a K–5 school located in a mixed socioeconomic area of predominantly working families. The philosophy behind this new approach, as stated in material promoting the program, was "Leveling the playing field between parent and teacher."

The first step was to fashion a suitable questionnaire to solicit a broader picture of home concerns. [See a sample at the end of the book.]

Questions ranged from the academic (What subject would you like to see your child improve in? What do you feel are his strongest areas?) to the personal (What makes your child happy? Is there anything currently making him sad?) to the parent-oriented (Are there ways you can contribute to the class? Will you want to also meet privately with the teacher?).

The initial conference was scheduled for close to the start of the school year, rather than deeper into October or November. "We wanted parents to enter the school in a more authentic way," Gayle explains. "We wanted them to know that this will be a parent-directed conversation."

Where the Tacoma model diverges from the usual is its emphasis on "action goals" plus a written "partnership plan" that is agreed to and signed by all parties. Teachers are trained to act more like social workers, probing, questioning, offering feedback, coaxing from the student and family a sense of their schoolwork priorities. Teachers are urged to ask families such questions as "What are your hopes for this school year?" and "What have been barriers in the past?", and they are counseled in techniques, such as paraphrasing, for improving communication with parents.

If, for example, math is cited as an area with room for improvement, the teacher will outline what the class will study over the coming months. From that, teacher, parent, and child will fashion a specific goal. For instance, learn the multiplication tables for numbers two to ten by Thanksgiving.

Sometimes the teacher suggests a goal that differs from the parent's. "If push comes to shove," says Gayle, "the parent wins."

These goals need only represent steps forward in a positive direction, not monumental accomplishments.

Kate Jensen's fourth-grade son, for example, came away from the winter conference (Larchmont teachers try to schedule at least three per year) with a resolve to try harder on his homework and to pay more attention in class. Toward that end, his teacher made a commitment to call on him more when he raised his hand in class. And the boy promised to make an effort to turn his body toward the front of the room.

Small steps perhaps, but a key idea behind the Partnership Conference is to have a practice in place that is comfortable to student, parent, and teacher. At minimum, it is there as a cautionary procedure, like a regular check-up by a good physician.

At maximum, parent, teacher, and student have fashioned a firm basis for working together.

....

Questions to Consider Asking the Teacher

The questions you choose to ask the teacher will obviously depend on your assessment of how your child is doing and the types of issues she's confronting. Some general ones to consider:

- What skills and knowledge should my child master this year?
- What kinds of tests has my child taken? What can be learned from them?

- How do you measure a child's progress? Through tests? Class participation?
- Is my child in any special groups? If so, for what reason?
- Are there things my child could benefit from by working on at home?
- What is your homework policy? What are the objectives? Is it graded?
- Is my child working up to her ability?
- How do you identify and adapt to learning style differences?
- Are there other children with similar aptitudes?
- Does my child have a friend or friends in the class? What can you tell me about them?
- How is my child's behavior? How has it evolved?
- Is my child talkative or quiet? How does my child function in groups?
- What do you see as my child's strengths and weaknesses? Examples?

Which questions you choose to ask and the emphasis with which you present them will have a lot to do with your perceptions of your child's special issues. This is another way of saying, the more insight you have into your child's school experience, the better able you will be to learn more from the teacher.

Is your child falling behind? Underchallenged? Beset with social problems or inhibitions? Or does everything seem to you to be just fine? Knowing which camp your child falls into can help direct your focus at the conference.

What to Tell the Teacher

These conferences are intended to be an exchange of information. Your child's teacher will likely be interested to know about:

- What your child has enjoyed about the class
- What your child has found difficult or confusing

- Learning style information that may not appear in your child's school file
- Stress at home that may impact your child
- Health or physical problems that could affect your child's performance
- Children in the class that your child enjoys
- Your child's impressions of homework assignments

Keep in mind that teachers don't mind hearing that they are revered and adored. But they also need to know if problems exist.

Concluding the Conference

If any suggestions have arisen, it's best to make sure you each understand what's to be done. Is there action you expect the teacher to take? Was anything discussed that merits a follow-up meeting?

Finally, you might consider asking the teacher if there are ways you can assist the class. Chaperone a field trip? Contribute project materials that are in short supply in this time of tight budgets? Supervise at the science fair?

The benefits (to the teacher, your child, and yourself) of volunteering at school cannot be overemphasized. If you have the time or inclination, the conference might be a good occasion to raise this subject. Teachers often maintain a checklist of their outside assistance needs, and this is a congenial way to learn more. Teachers know the acceptable boundaries regarding the sorts of assistance they can and cannot accept. It doesn't hurt to ask.

Should Your Child Attend the Conference?

I have not been an advocate of having students attend this conference. However, some new experiments with this practice are nudging me toward a reconsideration.

Most teachers and schools tend to discourage this. As I've stated, this conference has both an informational and a relational component. The presence of the child, in my estimation, can inhibit frank discussion between teacher and parent or guardian, and thereby undercut one of its major benefits.

That said, I can imagine situations, particularly when the objective is to really capture the student's attention, when being present at a discussion involving her parents and the teacher would make quite an impression. Underachieving students can often benefit from such a reinforced message.

The Big Picture

In my experience, these conferences work best if this *is not* the first time parent and teacher have met. It is easier to get down to the subtle and direct forms of communication if you have at least a passing impression of the teacher, and the teacher of you.

In the fall, there is the school open-house and other back-to-school occasions for you to get at least nominally introduced to the teacher. Also, many classrooms, particularly at elementary schools, offer various ways you can volunteer (see Chapter 16) to help out, in the library, on field trips, or with special projects. All these place you in proximity to the teacher.

I'd like to be able to say that teachers treat all parents with equal sensitivity and consideration. I believe that most certainly do try. But parents who are known to the teacher, especially if it's a parent who has helped out or somehow contributed, tend naturally to enjoy a familiarity that can lead to a more productive conference.

I fully recognize that many parents have very busy lives and may work long hours that preclude much of what I just prescribed. Certainly teachers, many of whom arrive at work at 7 A.M. and do not leave until after 5 P.M., can and do empathize.

It may be that the conference provides the only way for you to dialogue with your child's teacher. If so, I urge you to pay close attention.

Like a walk through the woods, there is much to be learned if your senses are attuned. And there's even more to be learned if you know what you are looking for.

10

Disabilities, Learning Disabilities, and the General Classroom

Mid-morning in an average public school.

In a first-grade classroom, an anguished child frenetically wrings his hands. A teaching aide tries to get him to calm down and focus on the blackboard, where the many uses of the letter "B" are being demonstrated to attentive children who don't seem to even notice the disruption.

Nearby, a third-grade class pauses imperceptibly in its discussion of amphibious creatures as four children file out. The students walk down the corridor to the resource room, where the reading specialist awaits them.

Elsewhere, as a fourth-grade class settles down for its history test, a girl drifts dutifully to a rear desk, clutching the text book. With no comment from teacher or classmates, she opens the book, laying the test alongside it, and begins answering the first question: Why did the pilgrims decide to leave England?

All the above situations involve children with disabilities, and the way these children are accommodated and incorporated into regular routines of the school can amount to a small miracle. When it works well.

If your child has benefited from any of its multifaceted services, you will not be surprised by the broad reach of the Individuals with Disabilities Education Act (IDEA).

161

If, however, you are new to public schools and your child is sharing his classroom for the first time with children who have disabilities, you may have questions about the situation. Children who were previously assigned to separate schools or isolated rooms are now taught, whenever possible, alongside the general school population.

And due to the sometimes tricky diplomacy that permeates this issue, your questions might be ones that nobody jumps up to answer.

What are the guidelines? What are the mandates? Who decides which children belong where? Most of all, what exactly does this mean for your child's schooling?

The most obvious feature about special education in today's school . . . is how much is, in fact, not obvious. Experts in the field freely refer to the two types of disabilities as **visible** and **invisible:** those that are observable and have traditionally been designated as such; and those that are, in effect, hidden but nonetheless profound.

This distinction gets to the heart of much of what is confusing about special ed. It's not exactly what you think. And it's not precisely what you see either. But it is, unquestionably, a unique and challenging feature of your child's school.

Inclusion—as the practice of involving children with disabilities in regular classrooms is called—is likely to have an influence on aspects of your child's schooling. My view of inclusion is that it's a grand opportunity and should be presented as such. The actual logistics, however, can sometimes be tricky.

If your child is eligible for the provisions of IDEA, you will encounter a ground-breaking world of tremendous promise. It is also a world that may demand quite a lot from you, including a crash course on educational jargon and a fair amount of bureaucratic gamesmanship.

If your nondisabled child finds himself in a classroom with children who appear markedly different, who are afflicted with impediments and disabilities that in your day rarely found their way into regular classroom settings, it's important for him to understand the bold challenge driving this policy.

That challenge is, quite simply, to put into practice what we like to preach about valuing all children.

What Is the Law and How Do Schools Interpret It?

IDEA directs public schools to provide a free, appropriate education to any child who qualifies as needing special education. The law goes on to state that "to the maximum extent appropriate" these students should be "educated with children who are not disabled."

The law also stipulates that the student receives a valid, unbiased test of the disabilities in question, and that the parent or guardians have an opportunity to be involved in decisions made about his education.

In essence, IDEA and a companion law, section 504 of the Rehabilitation Act, function as civil rights provisions for disabled persons.

The underlying belief of the IDEA '97 law (so named for the year of its reauthorization by Congress) is that schools should strive, as much as possible, to teach students with disabilities the same curriculum to the same standards as their nondisabled peers.

Moreover, students with disabilities are to be taught, wherever possible, within the general education classroom using appropriate teaching assistants and services, rather than in self-contained classes. This is the notion at the heart of what is known as *inclusion*.

The twin goals central to achieving this are:

1. To provide an *appropriate* education.
2. To do so in the *least restrictive environment*.

Generally, *appropriate* education amounts to a directive for schools to modify individualized instruction, rather than create one-size-fits-all remedies. Programs and services must, to a degree, be personalized and tailored for each child. The Individualized Education Plan (IEP) forms the centerpiece of this process.

"Least restrictive environment" means the situation where the child will most likely be successful. This is often interpreted to mean the general classroom, the setting that affords the most contact with nondisabled children. Thus, students with disabilities are to be educated separately or in isolated groupings only when their particular situation or problem makes it unfeasible to place them in the regular classroom.

Through a combination of modifications (to curriculum and instruction) and assistive technologies (like voice output computers), schools try to make the general classroom into the "least restrictive" placement for disability students. When this cannot be accomplished, schools still maintain separate resource rooms where students with disabilities can spend part or all of the day.

As to the eligibility of a child under IDEA, this is determined through tests and assessments performed by school and education professionals.

IDEA is a federal statute, and there is considerable variance in the ways that states, cities, and towns interpret and enforce its provisions. Some language and terms of the law are imprecise. Depending on the child, the classroom, and the school, there may be different interpretations as to how these concepts should be implemented.

Schools must comply. They cannot opt out due to budgetary or logistical obstacles. There have been lawsuits (and will be more) contesting what constitutes compliance. But schools tend to be generally supportive of the law, though sometimes wary of it.

IDEA can place schools in a complicated position and can assign them responsibilities they may not be completely equipped to handle. For IDEA to work well, schools need to have adequate resources for reducing class size, to offer additional training for classroom teachers in how to work with these children, and for planning time so staff can better coordinate the services some of these children may require.

What Disabilities Are Covered by This Law?

IDEA specifically covers the following disabilities:

- Mental retardation
- Hearing impairments, including deafness
- Autism
- Speech or language impairments
- Visual impairments, including blindness
- Orthopedic impairments
- Specific learning disabilities, including dyslexia, problems with visual and auditory perception, and ADD/HD

The definitions of the above disabilities in state and federal law can sometimes be confusing. If you're in an early stage of exploring whether your child is eligible, it's probably a good idea to check with school department specialists or advocacy groups that focus on disabilities in schools.

How Do You Determine if Your Child Is Eligible for Special Education Services?

Referral for evaluation.

The classroom teacher is primarily responsible for referring your child for special education evaluation. As I've noted elsewhere, not all teachers are trained in the subtle indicators of learning difficulties. Many have taken courses or attended workshops that provide an overview of early warning signs and what to look for, but some have not.

The teacher, however, does not have to be an expert at the fine points of diagnosis in order to know that a problem is worth further exploration. Most teachers know how to pick out children who are floundering in ways unrelated to effort or ability. The capable child who consistently performs poorly is a likely subject for referral. Many districts use a benchmark of two years—if your child's academic achievement in a subject area is two years or more behind what is considered age-appropriate, special ed testing is in order.

It does not always work that way. The teacher may not see it, or may attribute your child's problem to a simpler cause, like laziness or general developmental slowness. Remember: *You have the right to request that your child be tested for learning disabilities.* As in so many other areas of schooling, there is no substitute for a parent who pays attention to their child's learning. It is the single best assurance that the system will work well for your child.

If you feel that your child has a learning disability, and you believe so on the basis of careful observations, insist on formal testing.

Evaluation

Once a referral is made, a multidisciplinary "child study group" is convened (sometimes termed "school screening committee" or "educational management team" or other names), consisting of the teacher, a counselor or expert, the principal, the nurse, and other relevant specialists. The group's job is to make a determination as to whether the child is eligible for special education services.

You should be informed by the school if this step is being taken. In point of fact, the school will need your permission to test your child for disabilities.

This process can be intensely confusing. You may find yourself suddenly overwhelmed with information. The jargon is often mystifying and the array of possible tests is bewildering.

Adding to your consternation may be the urgency of the school's recommendations. They want to test your child and they'd like to do it soon.

You, of course, don't want to waste time. Yet you do not want to act hastily. Remember that you are your child's advocate. You will play an important role throughout this process, and it is only going to work smoothly if you feel comfortable with the approach that's been decided.

Ask questions. Come to the school for meetings. Consult other parents and advocacy groups. Read what you need to know to stay up to speed. Make sure you understand what is being proposed, and that you feel positively about it before giving your approval.

Testing will play a key role. The decision about what test or tests to administer is made by the school psychologist or resource specialist. Different tests hone in on different aptitudes. Some states regulate which tests can be given according to the suspected disability.

You should be informed about all aspects of your child's diagnostic testing:

- What tests will be given
- What the school hopes to learn from the test
- How much time the test will take
- When results will be known
- How to interpret results

There are a variety of tests that can be given. Different schools have their preferences. Some of the commonly used ones are:

- Woodcock Johnson: assessment of reading, writing, math
- Weschsler Intelligence Score of Children (WISC): tests cognitive functions
- Test of Auditory Perceptual Skills (TAPS): measures auditory processing
- Slingerland Test: used for diagnosing dyslexia and related visual and auditory skills

The process of having your child tested for learning disabilities can be confusing and anxiety-filled. You want to find out *something* and you secretly hope the test reveals *nothing*. In addition to which, you will need to explain to your child why this is being done and what the potential consequences might be.

Your child's special ed evaluation will, in addition to testing, also involve observations from the classroom teacher and your own input. These observations will help determine which tests are given as well as focus attention on areas too subtle for tests to detect.

It's a process that can take a toll on you and your family, but it is almost always valuable.

....

Relevant Facts:

- 10 to 15 percent of the school population qualifies for special ed
- The federal government had promised to provide 40 percent of the funding for IDEA's implementation; so far they have paid only 15 percent
- Dyslexia is the most common learning disability

....

Attention Deficit Disorder and Other Newer Classifications

In recent years, we have grown increasingly aware of a cluster of learning disabilities that might previously have been interpreted as behavior or personality problems. These "hidden handicaps" are neurologically based and can greatly impede an otherwise capable child's academic performance.

Learning disabilities are not the same as mental retardation, autism, deafness or behavioral disorders. They include:

- Dyslexia: difficulty in processing one or more areas of language, including reading, writing, and spelling
- Attention Deficit Disorder (ADD): difficulty in focusing and maintaining attention. Also, the related Attention Deficit Hyperactivity Disorder (ADHD)

- Specific Language Disability (SLD): severe difficulty in some aspect of language skills
- Visual Perception: difficulty in noticing and interpreting visual information
- Auditory Discrimination: difficulty in perceiving the differences between speech sounds
- Discalculia: severe difficulty in comprehending the symbols and functions for mathematics
- Dysgraphia: severe trouble in writing legibly and with appropriate speed

There is no single and reliable set of indicators for the early discovery of learning disabilities. Whereas teachers are clearly at the front line, not all teachers are trained in diagnosing the sometimes subtle signs associated with these disorders.

Furthermore, some children are adept at finessing their performance in a way that might, for a while, escape the teacher's attention. But you notice details the teacher hasn't yet picked up on—gaps in your child's reading comprehension, slowness to process verbal instructions, inversion of letters.

If you suspect that your child may have a learning disability, if you're the sort of parent who pays close attention to your child's learning and knows what comes easily for her and what requires a struggle, you are certainly in a position to be the one to sound the alarm. **Bring your suspicion promptly to the attention of the teacher.**

Increased awareness of the so-called "invisible" disorders is placing schools in ever more complicated situations. The fact that some of these disorders are hard to specify and detect creates a host of problems regarding diagnosis, treatment and classroom accommodations.

Classroom teachers, while striving to stay informed of the most recent discoveries and designations, may have a hard time distinguishing some of these newer disorders from more routine problems. This has been especially true with regard to ADHD.

Ask your principal and the counselor how your school deals

with these, in terms of evaluation, testing, and remedies. Also, many of the above-mentioned learning disabilities have national, regional, state, or even local advocacy associations (see page 196) which can be an excellent source of guidance and information.

• •

Beaverton, Oregon: Worried and Confused

In one key way, Joan Vicks of Beaverton, Oregon, was not a typical parent of a child with learning disabilities. As an educational consultant and former teacher, she knew quite a lot about the subject of learning disabilites.

In other respects, however, she was like so many other parents—worried and confused about her child.

When her son Nathan was in kindergarten, she noticed that he was slow to learn the alphabet. Mentioning this to his teacher, Joan was told, yes, that seemed to be the case. But the teacher hastened to point out that Nathan was bright, had an excellent vocabulary, and had plenty of company in the class. So Joan let it pass.

In first grade, she was bothered that Nathan seemed especially slow to grasp the basics of reading. She brought this to the attention of the teacher, who did not share her concern. Nathan's probably a late bloomer, she was told. He needs to try harder. Furthermore, the teacher pointed out that Joan might be inadvertently comparing Nathan to his older sister, a precocious student.

Joan acknowledged that she did sometimes fall into that trap, and let it pass.

In second grade, she noticed that Nathan was showing signs of reversing letters when he wrote. He was still slow to read. Again, she told the teacher of her worries, and was assured that Nathan was quite capable. Boys, she was told, can sometimes take longer to read. As for the letter reversals, the teacher said many students do that when they're young.

Third grade, however, was a level Joan knew well. She had taught at this level. She knew what kids should be able to do, knew the norms. Midway through the year, when Nathan was still floundering, she finally recognized that this was not just a phase he would grow out of. The situation was serious.

Joan insisted that Nathan be tested for learning disabilities. The teacher agreed and the school arranged for him to take the Woodcock Johnson and WISC assessment tests.

To Joan's disappointment, but not to her surprise, her son was determined to have a language learning disability.

Joan knew that the diagnosis needed to be more finely tuned. The Slingerland test, which is honed to detect dyslexia and related disabilities, was the one she wanted for her son. Her school, like many, did not have the expertise to administer it.

Outside testing can be expensive, as much as $1000 or more, depending on the credentials of the tester, the particularities of the tests, and the geographical region where you live. (Also, it's important to know if the tester's results will be accepted as valid by the school; some are not.)

The results came in. Not only was Nathan determined to be dyslexic, but, in Joan's words, "he was very dyslexic."

How could this have gone undetected for so long? She was angry at the teachers for failing to pick up the clues. But mostly she was angry at herself for being dissuaded from strong hunches about her own child.

She'd fallen into that most seductive of traps for a parent of a floundering student, wanting to believe that your fears are exaggerated and largely unfounded.

It was not until the next school year, fourth grade, that Nathan was able to receive special education services. Avid to make up for lost time, Joan was able to convince the IEP committee to approve a range of aggressive accommodations—pull-out sessions every day of the week to work on phonemic awareness, books on tape (when available) to help Nathan keep up with literature assignments, extra time for writing assignments, permission to take tests in the resource room under the supervision of the resource specialist.

Slowly, steadily, Nathan gained ground. Now in the sixth grade, his prospects are good. But to close the gap he needs to work hard. And will probably always have to do so.

In retrospect, was there anything—beside not backing down from her sharpest suspicions—that might have made a difference?

Joan thinks so. She believes there should be greater emphasis on providing regular teachers with a better background in basic special ed, particularly as a standard part of their teacher training. "Had those (first- and second-grade) teachers been better trained, we might have caught it earlier," she laments.

Interestingly, Nathan's second-grade teacher—the one who thought he'd grow out of it—did eventually attend a professional workshop on dyslexia. Joan, in her professional capacity, also happened to be there.

"He came up to me," she recalls with a sigh, "and said apologetically, 'wow, I guess I never realized how difficult it was for your son'."

. . . .

What Services Does the School Provide for Special Needs Students?

Once your child is deemed eligible for special education, the school is obligated—by law—to take measures to provide "a continuum of services" that will allow for ongoing and appropriate education.

What does this mean? In practical terms, the school is required to provide such tools and supplements as are deemed necessary to keep your child learning and to do so, to the maximum extent possible, in the context of the general classroom.

How are such seemingly ambiguous terms as "continuum of services" and "maximum extent" determined? In special ed, it is the Individual Education Plan, or IEP, that translates the rhetoric and good intentions into concrete action.

What Is an IEP?

The IEP is the critical instrument in the school's approach to helping your child. It sets the guidelines and timetables, and is a legal contract between the school and your child stipulating services to be provided. Elements included in the IEP must be adhered to.

The IEP amounts to an intervention strategy. As such, it represents the school's best assessment concerning the nature of your child's difficulties and what approaches hold the most promise. It is an attempt to marshall the collective resources and insights of the teachers and staff to create a custom-made plan for your child.

The shape and direction of the IEP—what the objectives are, what measures will be used to achieve them—will be hammered out at a conference attended by your child's classroom teacher, the school counselor, the resource specialist, possibly the principal or assistant principal, and you.

Your participation in the IEP process is extremely important. In essence, you are a partner in this process and you should view your role as such. Before the IEP plan can be implemented, you will be required to literally sign off on it, indicating your approval.

What Will the IEP Look Like and Contain?

In fashioning an IEP, teachers and staff are generally given broad flexibility to come up with creative solutions and approaches to your child's situation. The goal is to formulate a plan that allows your child to learn material learned by the general class, and do so in a similar time frame.

The accommodations and modifications stipulated in your child's plan can range from the familiar to the innovative. These can include:

- Regular sessions with a speech pathologist
- Easy access to assistive technologies
- One-on-one teaching aid
- More time for taking tests and quizzes

For example:

- A child with short-term memory disability may be allowed to use written notes during quizzes and exams.
- A high-functioning nine-year-old child with Down's syndrome who is normally situated in a special needs room should periodically participate in a first-grade class reading group.
- An ADHD child will be allowed to periodically leave the classroom and walk around during times of stress.
- A dyslexic child will be allowed to listen to books-on-tape in lieu of reading them.

You should view the IEP as the school's game plan for your child. As such, it should demonstrate the accumulated wisdom and creative problem-solving of education professionals, and should be specifically geared to your child. [See sample forms at the end of this book.]

Your Role in the IEP

You should never feel marginal to the IEP process. You will be involved both in the initial meeting to formulate the IEP, as well as subsequent meetings held at least once per year to review and revise the plan.

It cannot be overstated: Your role in the IEP process is vital. Teachers and counselors, of course, bring a level of insight and expertise that is critical. But the more diligently you participate, the more informed you can be about the nature of your child's disability and the array of options (and obligations) the school has, the better the IEP will serve your child.

You know your child better than anyone else. You know if the strengths and shortcomings that are discussed seem accurate. You may have anecdotal information to provide that will augment or even alter the IEP team's direction. You should be encouraged to come forward. In addition, you have the right to propose methods and modifications that you feel will serve your child.

If some element of the plan strikes you as ill-suited or wrong, don't be shy about questioning it. As Sharron McCarthy, a Sacramento, California, mother of a disabled child, recalls, "At first, it's so emotional because you're sitting there (at IEP meeting) and they're rushing you through because they have a tight schedule. But I soon realized: Hey, I only get once a year to do this, it's important, and nobody's going anywhere until I feel ready."

You will be meeting and communicating with educators and resource specialists who can often fall into a habit of using terminologies and referring to programs that are unfamiliar to you. You should bring yourself up to speed, as much as possible, with the language of special education services. Advocacy groups can help, and many local and state agencies provide printed literature explaining the services schools provide and the language affiliated with them.

The goals arrived at in the IEP report should seem reasonable to you, as should the methods for achieving them. When in doubt, ask:

- What new approaches will be used beyond what's been tried before?
- Will these steps be enough?
- If not, what else might we need to do?
- Are the timetables for achievement feasible?
- How is the effectiveness of the IEP to be measured?
- How frequently will you receive progress reports?

It's helpful to learn what has worked well for kids with needs similar to your child's. Networking with other parents and advocacy groups is an excellent way to do this. Other parents can also help brief you on the dynamics of the meeting and the types of information you'll need to have at your fingertips.

If you're uncomfortable playing a role of such consequence, or do not feel up to learning all you might need to know to play the role effectively, or have found past dealings with the IEP committee to be difficult, you might consider using an outside advocate to attend the IEP meeting with you.

This person can be either a trained professional—an educational therapist or psychologist—or another parent with appropriate experience. You can probably locate, through internet research or on recommendation of the school psychologist, a state or regional nonprofit advocacy group working in the area of your child's disability that can help you find a suitable advocate.

Schools are familiar with the concept of advocates. You need only notify them in advance that one will be attending with you.

Are General Classroom Teachers Prepared to Deal With Disabled Children?

The training and resources received by the teacher are key to the smooth functioning of a classroom containing disability students. An experienced and capable teacher knows how to maneuver and integrate the various IEP modifications without disruption, and can transform looming glitches into "teachable moments."

Most teachers, particularly newer ones, have had at least some training in the needs of children with disabilities and ways to manage a classroom. They are not likely, however, to have had much focused training in all the myriad disabilities they might be called on to handle.

If your child has a disability or is placed in a classroom with disabled children, it is appropriate for you to inquire about the teacher's training and background in this respect. Where possible, administrators assign students with disabilities to teachers who have successfully dealt with comparable situations in the past.

Regardless, the school should make available to the teacher a special education expert who possesses the proper knowledge and experience. This resource person will be assigned to help and advise the general education teacher in the intricacies of modifying instruction for the disabled learner. To do this without compromising the spirit and flow of the classroom takes considerable thought and effort.

When a disabled student is assigned to a general classroom, it is understood that the IEP team is responsible for overseeing the child's progress, that this is not exclusively the responsibility for the classroom teacher. As a practical matter, the classroom teacher often assumes the lion's share of the job, and it can indeed be large.

Parents are right to want to know if the teacher is up to the task. Likewise, teachers should be forthright with parents concerning the limitations of the classroom or any lack of services. Nobody is well served by pretending that a flawed situation is working just fine.

The theory behind inclusion is that when it is done right, it is an asset for everyone involved. When it is done poorly, people—disabled children, other children, and the teacher—can get hurt.

How Inclusion Impacts the Classroom

If your child is receiving special education services, you want the normal functions of the daily classroom to be flexible enough to permit those to occur. You want the teacher to be able to spend time with your child. You want the other children to be understanding of your child's differences. You want your child to have a fair chance at normal learning in the context of goals that are adapted to her disability.

If your child does not have a disability, you do not want the special services accorded to children with disabilities to interfere with your child's education. You want the teacher to be focused and unhurried. You want the classroom to run efficiently without undue disruption.

Both these objectives are possible. But they cannot be realized simply by wanting it to be so. Smooth implementation of inclusion requires a firm commitment of resources. These include:

- **Trained classroom assistants.** It's no secret that some children with disabilities can be needy and demand a disproportionate share of the teacher's time. The recommended ratio of aides to special needs students can vary according to the demands of the student. If you question whether your school is employing a suitable number of aides, you might seek an interpretation from the teacher, the principal, or an advocacy group. IEP plans often stipulate the presence of teaching assistants, and on what basis.

- **Release time for the teacher** to receive extra professional development or to attend workshops. Yes, many dedicated teachers have been and will continue to supplement their knowledge and skills on their own time, after school hours. But the best way to make inclusion work is for the teacher to be encouraged by the school system to pursue additional training.

- **Time for the teacher** to meet with the special education experts about the implementation of the IEP and assessment of how the child is doing. Again, teachers should be afforded time during the normal school day for such meetings.

- **Assistive technologies,** such as language boards, head pointers, and voice output computers, to enable students to communicate with the teacher and to learn at a pace parallel to the rest of the class.
- **Help for the teacher** in creating curriculum and lessons for special needs students. Counselors and outside experts can be called on to play a role here. Although some manage to pull it off heroically, busy and overworked classroom teachers cannot be routinely expected to devise new lesson plans aligned to the particular disabilities of special needs students.

Optimally, inclusive classrooms can operate to the advantage of the nondisabled student. Teachers who've been trained to adapt their techniques to hearing or visually-impaired students, for example, possess sharpened skills that can carry over to students with audio or visual learning style preferences. Teaching assistants with special skills are available to help others.

But without the commitment of adequate resources, the inclusion classroom can become a frenzied, beleaguered place where nobody gets what they want. Most schools understand this and are committed to doing their best.

Still, these adjustments can be costly and the school sometimes needs to be prodded. You should make certain that your school practices inclusiveness in a way that allows it to work—for everybody.

What if Your Child is Denied Services?

As your child becomes involved in the processes surrounding special education, there are bound to be instances where you object to or have strong reservations about what is being proposed.

This can range from disagreements about the severity of your child's condition to implementation of portions of the IEP.

Do you have any recourse? For the most part, yes.

For starters, if you believe your child should be eligible for special ed and a determination is made otherwise, you have the option of additional outside testing.

There are procedures in many states for having the cost of additional testing borne by the school district. But the process of getting approval can be complicated and lengthy. In all likelihood, outside testing will come at your expense (sometimes $1000 or more).

If the test is reputable and administered by a qualified professional, however, the results can (presuming they confirm your opinion) often force a reversal in the school's position.

Disagreement can also arise if you feel that the school is failing to follow through on some aspect of its obligation (not enough time in the general classroom, lack of an assistive technology, no pull-out session with a specialist, etc.). If that occurs, you have the right to appeal to a hearing.

What if You Disagree With the School's Placement of Your Child?

Quite simply, you do not have to permit your child to be placed in special education programs. The school has the right to appeal your decision.

As a practical matter, disagreements like this are usually settled through mediation.

Again, if the disagreement centers on a core evaluation of your child, it may be in your interest—and the school's—to seek additional testing.

What Is Appropriate for General Students to Know About a Classmate's Disability?

Many teachers find it useful to explain aspects of a student's disability, particularly if it is "invisible," to the class.

Such explanations can help foster empathy and understanding, and deflect feelings about special treatment or favoritism. When the general class population has a fuller grasp of the dilemmas of their special needs peers, the result in terms of improved classroom dynamics can sometimes be remarkable.

However, this should only be done with the explicit consent of the family of the disabled child. Some teachers will know how to approach this touchy and complex situation. Others may not.

Parents of disabled children should strongly consider making such a gesture. If you feel that your child's disability is insufficiently understood by his classmates, or that the class could benefit from a larger and more open discussion of it, you should consider approaching the teacher for a talk about ways this might be accomplished.

There are several options:

- You can appear before the class.
- You can authorize the teacher to brief the class.
- The resource specialist can brief the class.
- The teacher can present a "disability awareness" lesson.

The effectiveness of any of these steps, of course, depends on the sensitivity of your child and the unique dynamics of his relationship to her peers. I understand the temptation not to do and say anything. There is, however, a better way.

Common Misunderstandings About Special Education

It is an administratively cumbersome and logistically complex add-on to normal schooling. No. Special education is part of the school's proper and legally mandated responsibility.

These children are doomed to be stuck in problematic circumstances. In fact, many students exit out of special ed and continue on to "normal-track" schooling.

Special ed children are disruptive and not subject to normal standards of discipline. Special needs students are held to standards of conduct. They are not allowed in the regular class if they pose a danger to themselves or others. They are removed to a fully self-contained or separate class if they cannot adapt.

Special education takes precious funds from regular activities for the benefit of a small minority. Special needs students are children of the school district, with parents who live here and pay taxes. Studies have demonstrated that the cost of properly educating children with disabilities in public schools is a "good buy" for the district and for the society. In theory, full funding of special needs programs should not take away from general education. In practice, school districts often require supplemental funds to make special needs education work for everyone.

A disabled child has a legal right to inclusion. A child has a legal right to inclusion if, and only if, the IEP determines that to be the least restrictive environment appropriate for that child.

Special ed students are a big distraction to the classroom. Yes, some children with disabilities can require extra attention. But with appropriate support (teaching assistants, assistive technology, allowances for moving about and breaks), the class should function smoothly.

Learning disabled students are just slow learners. Children with learning disabilities either cannot learn the material or do so in highly irregular and unpredictable patterns. Slow learners simply take more time than others to learn material.

Rights of Parents of Children With Disabilities

IDEA explicitly grants parents of children with disabilities the right to participate in the decision-making process. This includes the right to:

- Free, appropriate education for your child
- Notification when the school wants to evaluate your child or change your child's placement
- Initiate an evaluation for special education or related services
- Request a reevaluation if you suspect your child's placement or services are not appropriate
- Obtain another, independent evaluation if you disagree with the school's evaluation
- Have your child tested in the language she knows best
- Participate in the development of your child's IEP
- Review all your child's records
- Have your child educated in the least restrictive school situation possible
- Request a due process hearing to resolve differences with the school

More detailed information about these rights, and the school's obligations, can be found at many of the websites listed at the end of this chapter.

The Big Picture

For all its complications and heartache, IDEA remains one of the great success stories of American public education. Twenty-five years ago, 90 percent of developmentally disabled children were housed in state institutions and about one million children with disabilities were shut out of schools altogether.

Today, 45 percent of children with disabilities are in the regular classroom, 5 percent are in a resource room or separate class, and fewer than 5 percent are in a separate facility. We are now educating more than 5.8 million disabled students in our public schools. And the number of disabled students graduating from our high schools and becoming productive members of society has been rising steadily for over ten years.

However, we need also to be mindful of the limitations of

IDEA. In the words of Ed Amundsen, former chair of the NEA's Caucus for Educators of Exceptional Children, the program exists "to level the playing field, not to provide a cure."

Schools can do a lot, but they cannot do it all. Schools can provide educational opportunities for children with disabilities that approximate the opportunities given to others. But we cannot remedy the sometimes profound disadvantages caused by those disabilities. And we cannot afford to ignore the potential disruptions caused by ineffective or poorly managed programs.

In far too many school districts, special needs children are put into regular classrooms without adjustments in the class size, without offering teachers additional training or technical assistance, and without allowing planning time.

Teachers and families are partners in this process. Inclusion—if you will indulge this veteran teacher a "teachable moment"—is an almost classic display of the basic principles of community and democracy.

Every individual student has a stake, a right to the best possible education. But what is good for one must be good for all. If we believe in the concept of inclusion, than we have no choice but to allocate the resources that allow it to work effectively.

Studies have shown that inclusion succeeds if there is thorough planning, if teachers receive adequate training, if class size is adjusted appropriately, and if additional staff and resources are available to assist in the regular classroom. Every one of those "ifs" wears a price tag. But there is, in my view, a steeper price to be paid by trying to implement inclusion on the cheap.

We should never lose sight of the goal. Inclusion done properly makes for a far richer learning environment for everyone.

WEBSITES

Families and Advocates Partnership for Education (FAPE)
www.fape.org
Learning Disabilities Association
www.ldanatl.org

National Center for Learning Disabilities
www.ncld.org
National Attention Deficit Disorder Association
www.add.org
International Dyslexia Association
www.idonline.org/index.html
National Information Center for Children
and Youth with Disabilities
www.nichy.org

11

Bullying and Harassment

We all know that the school environment is not ceaselessly harmonious. We know that children bring complicated emotional needs to school, and that the atmosphere can turn combustible. We know that kids get angry and spiteful and they make mistakes.

But bullying and harassment are another matter. As a teacher and a parent, my view of bullying and harassment has always been quite simple: It's unacceptable and it's wrong.

Bullying has no place in school. I have no patience for anyone who thinks that the cruel practice of bullying merely provides an unavoidable dose of "real world" toughening up for children. I have heard all the excuses for bullying and I do not buy any of them.

Why? Because precious lives are at stake. For students who are constantly picked on, ridiculed, or harassed, school becomes a living torture. Bullying exacts a terrible toll on children. Their schoolwork suffers. Their physical and mental health suffers. And the scars can last a lifetime.

The incidents are by no means limited to extreme or violent behavior. I recall a young girl who used to remain in my classroom long after the bell sounded, just lingering by desk. She was shy, maybe a bit nerdy. She was afraid to go out into the corridor. There were two older girls who constantly called her names and followed her in the hallway. Nastiness awaited her out there. She lingered by my desk because it was her one sure safe place. And I'd let her stay as long as she wanted.

The effects of bullying are serious, intense, and potentially long-lasting. For the victim, the ugliness of the incident may not, unfortunately, be the last or worst of the suffering. The humiliation and loss of self-esteem can radically alter how the victim interacts with peers and can negatively effect how peers view and behave toward him.

In the middle school where I taught, the girl I just mentioned was not the only victim. I would periodically witness harassment or be told of it by students. My first response was to approach the bully, always privately, and be absolutely direct: Do you know what you are doing? Do you understand that you are hurting someone? Do you realize the damage you're causing?

Sure, I'd occasionally get a smart-mouth answer in return. There were times when I had to contact a bully's parents or resort to other disciplinary measures to get a student's attetnion. But for the most part, I felt that I got through. It's amazing the impact a teacher can have on a child if the child knows that the teacher cares, and will hold the child accountable.

The children I confronted were never confused about my message. Bullying and harassment are—without exception—unacceptable.

And not only because of the damage done to the victim. Bystanders who witness such incidents are often beset with worrying whether they might become the next victim.

Bullying, it should be noted, is also bad for bullies. Tough and aggressive youngsters who never properly learn about consequences have a shaky future ahead of them. According to psychologist Dan Olweus in his ground-breaking work, *Bullying at School,* 60 percent of boys who had been identified as bullies in middle school had at least one criminal conviction by the age of twenty-four.

For the bully, who may think his actions will increase his social standing and popularity, the truth will sooner or later come as a rude surprise. The social pathology of bullying, if unchecked, can intensify into attitudes and habits that are distinctly unpopular and self-defeating.

What's more, although bully and victim are unique individuals, the ugly incident usually falls into a familiar pattern involving family, cultural, and peer group issues. Any lasting solution must require all parties—parents, teachers, staff and children—to work together as a team with a common goal.

What Is Bullying and Harassment?

There are various ways to define bullying and harassment, but the important thing to note is that *it can be defined*. Many schools have a written definition of bullying and harassment that is easy to understand.

In its essence, it is persistent and recurring behavior that is *not wanted* by the victim.

It is when a weaker, smaller, or more vulnerable person is hurt, harassed, badgered or intimidated by a more powerful person dedicated to that task.

It is when one or more persons subject another to unwanted behavior, ranging from taunts to threats to violence.

Name-calling and teasing, which are tremendously destructive and harder to prevent, are forms of harassment. In elementary schools, teasing is in fact the most common form of bullying.

Sexual harassment is a form of bullying.

Sure, a school's working definition of bullying may contain some legal ambiguities. But the point is, teachers and administrators know enough about it to take action. And despite their occasional denials, students—both victims and perpetrators—usually know what it is.

What If You Suspect Your Child Is Being Bullied at School?

A puzzling "code of silence" can pervade school situations when it comes to bullying. The facts of a situation may not leap to your attention, but can trickle out in subtle ways.

Here are some indicators that your child may be experiencing a problem with bullying or harassment:

- Unexplained injuries, scratches, or torn clothing
- Sudden reluctance to go to school
- Appears irritable and refuses to say what's wrong
- Sleeplessness, loss of appetite, nervous tics
- Frequent headaches and other physical complaints
- Sudden refusal to ride the bus

Yes, there are other possible interpretations of these signals. If, however, you suspect bullying, it's best to quickly find a calm, private opportunity to approach your child about it.

Remember, this is quite upsetting for your child to talk about, especially if he is in the early primary grades. He may decline to go into very much detail. There may be only so much you will learn directly, at least at the outset.

If your child is not forthcoming with you, it can be useful to talk to his close friends or their parents, who may have helpful information.

Of course, the most important place to take your suspicions is to the classroom teacher or another school authority. Or, the school might inform you.

If and when that call comes, you can assume that the school has good reason to believe an incident has occurred and your child has already interacted with the teacher or school staff.

Important things to heed:

1. Time matters. Bullying is not a situation to let linger longer than it already has. The school should be told whatever information you possess—where the incident occurred, who was involved, whether you believe it is a singular event or part of a pattern, etc.
2. Tell your child that this *is not* supposed to happen, that it is not permissible, and that he or she *does not* deserve it
3. Instruct your child that the way to fight back *is to inform* the school authorities about what took place, and not engage in physical retaliation, threats, or other forms of revenge.

4. Assure your child that you will make sure that the school follows up on this, and puts an end to it.

Keep in mind that many children who are victims of bullying refuse to confide in parents. Being a victim of bullying can trigger shame, resulting in a secretiveness you might have previously thought unlikely in your child.

Part of the reason that children are reluctant to divulge the fact that they're being bullied is that they are skeptical that anything can be done about it. Moreover, they fear that telling could only make matters worse.

Children fear being subjected to further derision as a "tattletale." Shy or less assertive children—the type most commonly victimized—worry about exacerbating the estrangement they already feel. Plus, a standard tactic of bullies is to warn their victims never to tell, or else.

Remember that the most important goal of many children is finding a peer group. Some young people, particularly early adolescents, will do almost anything to fit in, including remaining silent about their own abuse.

What Should You Expect from the School?

The old boys-will-be-boys attitude about roughhousing in schools is very much on the wane. Teachers, principals and staff—like other parts of society—are quickly coming up to speed in their appreciation of the severity and scope of bullying and harassment. An increasing number of schools have written policies and warnings, and periodically dedicate an assembly or all-school workshop to the topic.

Schools are reluctant to play the role of judge and jury. Teachers can be slow to respond to perceived harassment either because they lack the time and resources to properly deal with it or they may be at a loss as to what to do. Nonetheless, the school is fully obligated to try to put a prompt end to a bullying situation.

When an incident occurs, teachers and school staff should:

- Step in and stop it immediately, no questions asked (getting the "two sides" to the story can wait until later).
- Remove the audience (i.e. other students) from the scene
- Act promptly in talking to the victim and the bully, and do so separately
- Contact the parents or guardians of the bully and the victim
- Communicate with other teachers, administrators and staff to share insights and advice
- Maintain communication with parents until the situation is resolved

If bullying occurs on school property or en route to or from school, the school is responsible.

Schools, however, can become defensive about the circumstances, particularly if there was a lack of supervision which could have allowed the bullying to take place.

If you're forced to intervene on behalf of your victimized child, you should set aside, at least initially, any accusatory tone. Questions such as "aren't the children being watched?" and "doesn't anybody monitor the hallway?" can be addressed after the immediate problem has been dealt with.

When you meet with the school, you should:

1. Make it known that you intend to monitor what they do and insist that they be accountable directly to you. The principal, in particular, should understand that you expect an immediate end to the situation, as well as ongoing monitoring to prevent a recurrence.
2. Convey any insights you have about your child, such as alienation and insecurity, that could be exacerbated by bullying. Also, convey any knowledge you have about the situation that might help the school address the problem.
3. Remember that schools really do have an unwavering commitment to a safe and worry-free environment. Your

goal is to make sure they act on what they believe. Respect the authority and expertise of the teachers and staff, and remind them that your child's safety depends on them.

4. Be mindful that the school is likely to sympathize with the victim's harassment and, on the other hand, feel some responsibility—and guilt—for having allowed it to take place.

5. Emphasize that you believe there is more to be done than simply catching the culprit, that the lasting solution you seek will necessarily join the victim, the bully, and others students in the resolution.

You may find yourself frustrated by the school's failure to act swiftly, or by the vagueness in their response. At some point, you may be justified in taking your complaint to higher authorities (the school superintendent, the school board) especially if you encounter any of the following attitudes among the school personnel or principal:

- Dealing with bullies is a normal part of growing up.
- Ignoring it is probably the best response.
- Your child will get over it.
- Your child's weakness and timidity contribute to the harassment.
- The school lacks the resources to deal with problem.

"Parents have to be prepared to be advocates and activists," advises Nancy Mullen Rindler of Wellsely College's Center for Research on Women. "A lot of times you're better off if you come forward with the PTO group."

Will Your School Conduct an "Inquiry" into Bullying and Harassment?

It is not necessary for the school to have a "provable" case for it to take the steps necessary to restore safety and establish some corrective measures. Your child will be asked to come forward with whatever relevant information he or she possesses. But this should be done in a manner that is gentle and not overtly investigative.

The school's approach to the bully will vary depending on past history.

Owning up to misdeeds is no easier for bullies than for other children. Bullies tend to be skillful at denying responsibility or shifting it onto other circumstances, i.e. the victim started it, someone else did it, or the standard, "it was an accident."

Bullies, for the most part, are children with some personal problems. It is entirely possible that a bully will, even if there are ample witnesses, deny the incident or cast it in a context skewed to justify what he did.

Teachers and school administrators are used to this, and usually know ways around it. Even the toughest grade school bully is usually far from a savvy criminal.

Teachers and school staff often have a pretty good idea of what's going on long before an incident is brought to their attention. Only when a report appears improbable, when it flies in the face of all prior understanding about the victim and bully, and if the incident is fairly serious (involving physical injury, for example, or a sustained campaign) will the school embark on a course that resembles an investigation.

This "investigation" might entail follow-up interviews, discussion with bystanders and other students, and additional meetings with parents of both bully and victim.

Even then, the school may not be overly determined to establish a certifiable picture of what is alleged to have taken place.

"Resolution is what we're after," asserts one veteran principal, referring to the desire for a satisfactory end to the harassment. "We don't need a full and accurate picture of all that took place in order to get there."

Monument, Colorado: Bullyproofing the School

Jes Raintree, a mother of two, had recently moved to Monument, Colorado, a fast-growth community neighboring Colorado Springs. Like many parents of children entering public schools, she made a special effort to keep her ear close to the ground, trying to learn what was really going on at the school.

Her children at the time were second graders. When they came home each day from the Ray Kilmer Elementary School, Jes would quiz them about their day. What happened? Who did you play with? What did you learn? The usual stuff. Also, she made a point of speaking frequently with other parents, mostly mothers, about what they learned from their children. And, of course, she visited the school often, attending the public meetings and parent nights. As a former high school teacher, Jes knew that the real truth cannot be fully contained in newsletters and principal's reports. What Jes learned was that bullying and harassment, sometimes invisible in the classroom, was widespread elsewhere.

One day her son came home with a bloody nose, the result of a tussle on the bus over a toy.

In school visits, she would routinely hear name-calling and nasty comments. And these were ostensibly "nice" kids from "good" families.

Jes investigated further. She spoke with other parents, quizzed them about their children's experiences. She was not surprised to learn that this pleasant school had a somewhat darker side.

"The kids were doing all right in class," Jes recalls finding out. "But they weren't doing well in the hallways and the cafeteria. And they really weren't doing well on the playground." Jes noticed a lot of physical aggression, a lot of angry voices. This concerned her and she decided to take action.

She approached the school principal. They talked. Jes learned of a bullying training workshop that was being offered near Denver. She proposed to attend, on the school's behalf, if the school paid her way. The principal thought it was a good idea, and agreed.

At the workshop, Jes was introduced to the basic tenets of Bullyproofing Your School training, a formalized method for creating a "caring majority of students who take the lead in establishing a safe school community." The program focuses on converting the silent majority of students by teaching strategies to both avoid victimization and to take a stand against bullying and harassment.

The full-day workshop, which cost $130, covered staff training, parent support, intervention with bullies, and techniques for cultivating a more caring school climate.

Most everything Jes learned at the Denver workshop impressed her as reasonable, and well worth attempting. The ambitious idea behind Bullyproofing Your School is to mount a counterforce of good practices and raised consciousness to combat a culture that increasingly glorifies hotheadedness, spite, and insolence. This is no small task, indeed.

Returning from the workshop, Jes Raintree and another parent, Brenda Eberhart, together received permission from the principal to launch the first step of Bullyproofing, an introductory training of the school's teachers and staff before the start of school in August.

When school started in the fall, the two mothers began implementing the steps of the Bullyproof program in the K–5 classrooms, once a week for half an hour over five consecutive weeks. These sessions touched on clear definitions of bullying, the elements of conflict resolution, how to respond to teasing, distinguishing tattling from telling, etc.

Each session allowed time for children to share their stories and engage in role playing exercises.

Also, Jes arranged ongoing activities designed to keep fresh the spirit of the lessons. Awards were given, in class and at assemblies, for exemplary conduct like befriending a child new to the school or helping someone who dropped their lunch tray. Each morning, a daily Bully Blurb, consisting of anecdotes or sayings ("Be someone your classmate can count on," "Name calling does not make anyone feel good") is read over the school intercom to the entire school.

The Bully Blurbs and almost all the other details of this program were the work of Jes and Brenda. Jes estimates that she spent some 4,000 hours over a two-year period on the project.

The program proved successful and popular. The reasons, according to Jes, are basic. "It provides options to the kids who are victims. It gives voice to the ones who've always been bystanders. And it takes the arena away from the bullies."

After the initial year, the program was requested by the district's three other elementary schools and the middle school. A dozen new parents were trained to handle these jobs. This was a completely voluntary parent-sponsored program at virtually no cost to the taxpayers.

The high school is their next target.

Was human nature altered by volunteer parents? Jes Raintree will certainly not go that far. She is, however, convinced that "bullying and harassment are controllable. And through that control, change happens."

Can the School Protect Your Child Against Revenge for Informing?

A critical myth about bullying—critical because it plays such a key role in the psychodynamics—is that the victim who "tells" on his oppressor leaves himself vulnerable to revenge and further harassment. Quite simply, this is a story perpetuated by bullies for the explicit purpose of concealing what they have done. The facts are different.

When school authorities handle bullying effectively, retribution rarely takes place. Clearly the operative phrase here is "effectively handle."

It is well within the powers of most schools to implement protections for the victim who comes forward. You should definitely make it a point to review with the teacher or principal what steps they intend to take along these lines, and you should hold them to it.

Successful resolution of a bullying incident must include an enforceable strategy for discouraging the bully, or his associates, from doing anything that can be interpreted as revenge.

Such a strategy can include:

- Letting the bully know there will be escalating consequences for repeat behavior
- Close monitoring of the bully and of the locations where the bullying took place
- Letting the parents of the bully know
- If this is part of a pattern of behavior, local police can be notified and called in to meet with the bully.
- Helping the bully understand the effect his behavior has on others
- Making sure your child knows that the school will not ignore this, and that the bully will be confronted
- Making sure your child knows that informing the school is a courageous thing to do, and you are proud of him for doing so

- Taking steps to involve other parents in an expanded discussion of the roots of bullying and harassment without making the incident a focal point

What if the Bullying Occurs on the Bus or the Walk Home?

Bullying tends to take place in the gray areas, where adult supervision is absent or diminished, and the student population is shifting or in flux. Counselors who work on bullying and harassment will sometimes issue students, as a research method, a map of the school campus and ask them to shade in the areas where they do not feel safe. Those places usually are washrooms, hallways and locker banks, recess areas and playgrounds.

Additionally, the school bus and the walk to and from home are singled out as locations ripe for this sort of problem. In each of these settings, it is difficult for the school to create a remedy using its standard means of increasing the presence of adult monitors. Moreover, it is harder for schools to investigate and intervene in these situations.

Nonetheless, the school remains responsible for the safety of the students "from portal to portal." Obviously this is best achieved through cooperation with parents in the larger community.

Any harassment on the bus should be reported to the principal, and you should approach the school with the same set of expectations you would have if the incident took place in the classroom.

Realistically, however, the school is less able to remedy bullying and teasing on the bus. Drivers may not be trained in ways to deal with bullying. And their attention is obviously focused elsewhere.

Some districts have video surveillance cameras installed on the bus to screen for incidents. But these tapes are generally not reviewed unless an incident is being examined.

Bullying that occurs on your neighborhood sidewalks and

streets in the course of commuting to school presents different problems. Here there is no formal adult presence. If there is anyone else around beside your child and the bully, it is generally other children.

If you know how and where the bullying occurs, you may have no choice but to be available onsite—or have other parents or guardians available—to discourage it.

Another offsite bullying opportunity that is only recently coming to light is the "instant messaging" feature of home email communication. With alarming frequency, this medium is playing a role both in fomenting and exacerbating harrassment of targeted students in ways that are invisible to parents and teachers. "Stuff that's brewing at school gets continued by this means after hours," points out Bill Benigni, a Bedford, Pennsylvania, school counselor. "Kids come in the next day and they're even angrier."

....

Relevant Facts

- Seventy-five percent of children are bullied or harassed at some time during their school career.
- More than 60 percent of victims report that the schools respond poorly, or never.
- The majority of victims feel they are picked on solely because they are weaker or smaller.
- Statistically, schools are the safest places for children to be, safer than home, safer than neighborhood streets and playgrounds.
- Sixty-five percent of bullying is done by boys, 15 percent by girls, 20 percent by boys and girls.
- The percentage of children being bullied is highest in elementary school.
- In middle school, the number of incidents diminishes but the severity increases.

- Bullies are among the most popular boys in school from the fourth to sixth grade

....

What Will the School Do to the Bully?

The following measures may be taken toward the bully:

- Be supervised during recess
- Have privileges, such as recess or after school privileges, taken away
- Parents brought in for a meeting
- Have local police or mental health counselor meet with the bully and family
- Switch the class or even school assignment
- Suspension from school
- Assign additional school time, after school or on Saturdays

Are There Preventive Measures That a School and Classroom Teacher Could—and Should—Take?

Bullying seems to flourish most where it *is not* featured as part of the regular school conversation. For this reason, it is sometimes referred to as "the evaded curriculum."

Bullying thrives in shadows and secrecy. Exposure is its enemy. Bringing bullying into the open is the most powerful preventative. Any school with a problem—and there are few without it—should have programs in place to address this.

Jerold Newberry of the NEA has developed a five-step method for teachers involving the entire class in discussing and solving the problem of name-calling.

1. Ask if anyone in the class has ever been called a name they didn't like.
2. Compile a list of those names.

3. Going down the list, ask students how they would feel if called that name.
4. Reach an agreement to stop using these names.
5. Reach an agreement on appropriate penalties for anyone who uses these names.

Other measures which have shown some success in reducing the incidence of bullying and harassment:

- Having an explicit policy with clear definitions that students understand
- Making bullying a topic of school-wide discussion and concern in classrooms and assemblies
- Adult monitoring of common spaces, such as hallways and playgrounds and washrooms
- Training of teachers and staff in what to look for and how to intervene
- Master/veteran teachers demonstrating techniques for newer teachers
- Encourage and exchange of information between classroom teachers and adult monitors about students and situations to watch for
- Appoint a contact person who is available to be contacted regarding complaints or information
- Inviting children to help formulate clear rules against bullying and harassment
- Focus on cooperative activities which reduce the isolation of shy or marginalized children (potential victims)
- Activities like reading selections and role playing that educate students about why children bully, and the hurt it causes

Do Incidents of Bullying Say Something About the School?

Isolated cases say very little. As I mentioned before, bullying is pervasive and crosses all lines of geography, class, and ethnicity.

It occurs in large schools as well as small, in wealthy districts as well as impoverished ones.

That said, a school that experiences repeated incidents of bullying, and has done so for several years, has a lot to answer for. There are many effective programs (see listing of websites) and models that a school can learn from.

If bullying incidents have occurred, there is almost no excuse for the failure of a school to implement most, if not all, of the preventive measures mentioned previously. Parents should press to know:

- Does your school have a program of bully awareness?
- Do teachers make a point of encouraging the class to bring bullying to their attention?
- Do the classroom teachers take extra steps to ensure an inclusive environment that encourages students to respect each other's differences?
- Are adults prominently present in the school's public spaces?
- Are staff members trained to identify bullying when they see it?
- Does the school board have policies and procedures stipulating meaningful penalties for bullying?

How Schools Respond to Violence

Schools, like other social institutions, are increasingly prepared to respond to violence and threats of violence. Are they adequately patrolled and policed? For the most part, no, and we would not want them to be.

Most schools have a plan for how to respond when a student acts violently or threatens violence. The basic features are to isolate and neutralize the perpetrator; shield other children from harm; notify the police; and notify the student's family.

School programs for violence prevention are similar to what you find for the prevention of bullying and harassment. They emphasize the identification of early warning signs and intervention to alleviate the situation.

Despite a spate of highly publicized incidents, schools remain perhaps the safest place for children to be. When these incidents do occur, they are almost always followed by the questions, "Why didn't we see it coming?" "Why didn't we pay attention to the signs?"

Here are some mental health warning signs that experts advise parents, teachers, and other children to pay attention to. (Note: these signs do not form an ironclad checklist, and none of these traits is necessarily a predictor of violent behavior.)

- Severe feelings of isolation
- Excessive feelings of rejection or persecution
- Being a victim of violence
- Extreme anger, physical fighting, and bullying
- Expression of violence or threats of violence in writings or drawings
- Intense prejudice
- Destruction of property

Schools are prepared to intervene if:

1. A student has expressed a specific intent and plan to harm or kill others
2. Is carrying a gun or weapon

Most experts agree that the single best way to reduce or defuse situations of potential violence is for students to have a meaningful and positive relationship with an adult. Whether that person is the current teacher, former teacher, counselor, administrator or staff person, what matters is that the student know there is someone at school who understands and can be trusted to care.

That, of course, is something schools should do anyway, and not just to prevent violence.

What Can You Do to Help?

There are various ways for parents, rather than be relegated to prodding the school from the sideline, to play an active and fore-front role in improving bullying and harassment conditions. You can:

- Participate in developing school rules and policies (Many schools are in the process of reviewing and revising their approach, due partly to an upsurge in incidents and enhanced awareness.)
- Volunteer to monitor trouble spots at school
- Receive training, similar to that given to faculty and staff, about detecting and dealing with bullying and harassment
- Meet informally with other parents to discuss these issues
- Most important of all, take special efforts to maintain an open dialogue with your child about what goes on at school that adults do not see

The Big Picture

School violence has been declining for over a decade. Studies show that children feel safer in school than they have in the past. Nevertheless, we live in a sometimes violent society and schools are vulnerable to the spillover.

As even casual observers of current events are aware, many of the recent outbursts of school violence have been directly or indirectly traceable to retaliation for physical or verbal bullying. Nobody can be pleased that bullying and harassment have made it onto the front pages of our newspapers and occupy the fore-front of our consciousness. The reasons this has occurred are indeed tragic.

I do, however, believe that this heightened awareness presents us with an opportunity. Bullying may have roots in so-called human nature, but it certainly seems to blossom in a culture of meanness and aggression. There is no redeeming value in allowing this environment to persist, and I am convinced we can change it.

How?

The place to start is at home. Study after study has shown that bullying behavior is frequently an imitation of aggression and insensitivity witnessed or experienced at home. A school can only do so much to alter bad habits that have been cultivated, and continue to be cultivated, in the home a child returns to every day.

The community also has an impact. By "community," I mean the other adult figures—neighbors, store keepers, sports coaches—with whom a child routinely interacts, as well as institutions like religious groups and social clubs that contribute to a child's understanding of values. Do these individuals and groups step in when a child acts with cruelty? Do they make the sometimes awkward and unwanted gesture of standing up for what is right?

I would hope so. But I fear that on the streets and at the parks and in the neighborhoods, behavior that is plainly intolerable is quietly tolerated. Amidst such influences, which not incidentally includes a deluge of desensitizing images from a crass mass media, schools are challenged to try their best.

It's sometimes pointed out that teaching "values" is not the role of schools. Well, schools might not offer a formal course titled "values," but we certainly should teach it. Anything less is negligent.

I believe it is possible to change the school culture from one where a bully can score points with his peer group by causing a weaker child's pain to one where the bully is rebuked for such behavior.

For the most part, I refrain from haranguing people toward deeper forms of activism and involvement. But it strikes me that parents should recognize that creating a more humane social environment is the best way—the only way—to ensure the future well-being of their children.

As if we needed any further reason to try our best to put an end to this syndrome, in recent years there have been a number of headline-grabbing incidents of bullied and tormented boys coming to school with guns, bent on revenge for past abuses. When such outbursts of violence occur, we are painfully reminded that the victims of bullying are not so easily limited to the solitary suffering child.

We are all its victims.

WEBSITES

Safe Schools/Healthy Students Action Center *www.sshsac.org*
NEA Safe Schools Manual *www.nea.org/issues/safescho/ssmanual.pdf*
Protecting Students from Harassment and Hate Crime
www.ed.gov/pubs/harassment/
Facing History and Ourselves *www.facing.org*

BOOKS

Bullying at School by Dan Olweus, Blackwell
Quit It!: A Teacher's Guide on Teasing and Bullying
by Froschl, Spring, and Mullin-Rindler,
NEA Professional Library

12

The A,B,Cs of Report Cards, Grades, Reading, and Math

Most public schools will issue report cards or grades between two and four times per year. Some schools do not begin this practice until a student is in grade three or higher. Others begin as early as kindergarten, but use narrative forms of reporting and then switch over to grades a few years later.

Like it or not, these reports will have a big impact on you and your child, and it's important for both of you to understand what they do and do not represent.

The process of deciphering the meaning of these reports is made more complicated by the fact that different teachers attribute different meanings to them, and often employ quite individualized systems for issuing marks.

Thus, the report card can:

a) provide additional information about how your child is doing;

b) provide significant new disclosures which come to you as a complete surprise;

c) be a duplication of what you already know;

d) all of the above.

The dilemma regarding report cards and grades is this: They are notoriously imprecise instruments; and they are also important. Teachers need them. Students need them. Parents need them.

But knowing what we need them for is not so simple.

Interpreting Your Child's Grade

Grading terminology can sometimes be complicated. Simpler systems employ numbers, 1–5, or the traditional letters, A–F.

Many schools, particularly in the lower grades, utilize words or phrases that can be somewhat nebulous but attempt to attach a more defined value to the grade. Here you might find—and the phrases differ greatly from district to district—such terms as, "emerging," "satisfactory," "excellent," "improving," etc.

You'll likely have questions about what this all means. Few of the markings are entirely self-explanatory. The report card itself will often contain a definition of terms. Teachers are keenly aware of the stated guidelines and they make an effort to subscribe to them.

Needless to say, teachers are also keenly aware of all that a grade omits or overstates. Teachers know that grades are but one means, and rarely the best means, of assessing a student. But school systems require grades, and teachers issue them.

As a consequence, most teachers have evolved an individualized—and sometimes highly individualized—system of adapting the formal definition of the grade to their own more subjective value system. What teachers try to do is create a grading system that constitutes a record of progress and motivates students to do well.

Teachers try to establish a grading system that is, above all else, based on high standards, flexible, and fair. And it's important that this system have credibility in the minds of the students. Grades should not be given on a "curve" basis, which predetermines that some part of the class gets a high mark, some part a low mark.

You'll be a rare parent if you don't find yourself wondering how other children of comparable abilities were rated. Did *everyone* receive a "B," a "2," a "satisfactory," a "need improvement"?

Comparisons aside, what you really need to know is:

- What achievement, or lack thereof, does the grade measure?
- Is the grade based on meeting a goal?
- Is the grade based on making progress toward a goal?
- How, for example, is the student who stays at the top of the class without really improving graded?

Teachers are usually willing to explain the meaning of a grade—but only up to a point. Remember that most teachers freely admit that their system is imperfect, mixing together several variables.

Many of the grading forms contain space for written comments by the teacher. Here is where you'll hopefully find reference to aspects of your child's performance that were not reflected in the actual grade.

These comments can be explicit or subtle, depending on the teacher's sensibility. They can cover anything from specific academic issues ("excels at seeing the concept underlying math problems") to personal behavior ("would be a better student if he listened more in class").

How Important Are Report Cards and Grades?

Children should have a clear idea of the importance the teacher places on grades, and what importance you place on them.

My own belief is that grades mean more as a target for students to strive for than as an ultimate measurement of how they have performed.

Whereas it is hard to predict ahead of time how your child will do in a reporting period, something is wrong if your child's grade catches you utterly by surprise. If this proves to be the case, then:

- You should be in closer touch with how your child's doing, or

- The teacher has failed to indicate to you how your child is doing, or
- The grade is seriously inaccurate.

There can be consequences to how your child does on report cards. Some schools practice forms of ability grouping and your child's grades might play a role in what teachers they are assigned to, and which other students are placed in the class with them.

Not until high school, however, will report card grades begin to have a cumulative and "lasting" importance. Slippage in elementary school, although it should certainly be avoided, can be rectified with no lasting scars.

An additional point about grades: Good teachers strive to create a grading system that will be perceived by kids as rigorous and fair. It is the teacher's hope that even a student who receives a poor grade will be enhanced, and educated by it.

What You Should Know About Curriculum

You will probably be baffled about exactly what it is your child is supposed to learn at each grade level, and what constitutes a reasonable pace for her to be learning it.

It's not vital that you be intimately informed of the curriculum your child is being taught. It may be that your child will be such an accomplished and self-sufficient student that it will make no difference, one way or the other. But it can be a different matter if your child is struggling or simply needs you to be a sympathetic—and somewhat informed—listener. But there are several reasons why you might want to know at least some details.

1. To be able to assist and support your child's studies, and know what she's talking about
2. To be better able to identify academic problems if your child is falling behind

3. To monitor how the curriculum is altered or adapted to fit the demands of standardized tests

Some parents like the chance to relearn (or learn for the first time!) what exactly prompted the Pilgrims to take the bold leap out of England. Other parents rely on their ability to either know what's needed (fleeing religious persecution) or to deftly steer the discussion into comfortable territory.

Many parents are content to know only what the outline of their child's class will broadly study: our early colonies during the early fall, then on to the Revolutionary period and culminating in the spring with a view of the nation at the brink of the Civil War.

There are several reasons that it helps for you to be informed:

- It shows that you care, and allows you to have conversations with your child that can be both instructive and fun.
- It allows you a more meaningful communication with the teacher about your child's performance.
- It connects you with other parents who may have concerns with what their child is being taught.
- Curricula is at the core of what school is about; knowing some things about it is useful to your understanding and appreciation of the school.
- There are two areas, reading and math, where your involvement may prove very important.

Beyond the elements of what your child is learning in various subject areas, there is another aspect to curriculum that might be worth your attention:

Is the curriculum created at the school, or is it a commercial product acquired from an educational publisher?

Many of the "off-the-shelf" curricula are quite good and provide teachers with a tightly organized, sequential approach to subject areas. Usage of these is on the upswing, in part because they offer a seemingly streamlined and systematic way to align curriculum with state standards.

Concerns about off-the-shelf curricula center around the rigid, lock-step nature of some of the packages and the way they can restrict teacher flexibility. As one veteran teacher put it, "If you don't allow teachers to be thinkers and problem solvers, how the heck are you going to have kids who are thinkers and problem solvers?"

You should ask:

- Is the curriculum "off the shelf", i.e. acquired from an educational publisher?
- Does the curriculum strive to teach both information and skill, understanding as well as facts?
- Have other comparable schools used this and been happy with it?
- Is your child's teacher free to decide what activities to use with different students or are the teacher's instructional decisions based on the demands of the program?

Is Information About the Curriculum Accessible?

Schools and teachers are generally quite open with parents about what it is they're teaching, or intending to teach.

You ought to have no difficulty learning the broad guidelines for what your child is being taught, not simply over the course of the year or the semester, but even—if you're interested—on a week-to-week basis.

You can learn a lot about curriculum:

- At the annual parents night or during your parent-teacher conference
- By checking your child's folders, notebooks, and textbooks
- By monitoring your child's homework assignments

- From posted lessons plans and curriculum information on the school website

Also, many school districts publish grade-by-grade curriculum guidelines, which you can obtain from the superintendent's office or online.

Can You Influence Curriculum?

Beyond a stray suggestion here and there to the teacher (not always welcome), there is little you can do to impact curriculum. In fact, as standards and standardized testing come to occupy a larger role, teachers find themselves with less and less influence over curriculum.

If you have serious concerns—or suggestions—regarding curriculum (i.e. the way math is taught, the emphasis on one aspect of science over another, the dropping of drama and art, etc.) the place to register these is not with the teacher. You may find that the authority over content in the classroom rests largely with the school superintendent or, to a surprising degree, the state board of education.

Staying on Top of Your Child's Reading

Through the third grade, goes the adage, your child is essentially learning to read. From fourth grade on, he will be reading to learn.

Either way, reading is the crucial, fundamental cornerstone of all that your child will accomplish, or attempt to accomplish, during his school career. Success in reading will yield successes in other areas. Problems in reading can ripple throughout all your child's scholastic efforts.

Your role in your child's reading is absolutely vital. Studies have shown that one of the best predictors of a child's success in school is the amount of time a parent or guardian spends reading to him. Home is where children should receive their first intensive exposure to reading. Doing so helps connect the act of reading to a parent or guardian, reinforcing the value of it.

In school, your child will encounter a reading environment that is different from his customary spot on your lap or the sofa. We hope this new environment will still involve some of the same feelings of comfort and nourishment. There will be an additional element though: teacher expectations.

In school, your child will be expected to learn in a sequential manner leading to a series of goals. Your child will be doing this in the company of other children. Not only will reading play a critical role in your child's academic development, but it will likely affect his self-image.

If you need to pick and choose where you can devote your time and attention concerning your child's schooling, this is the area that unquestionably makes the greatest impact. It can't be emphasized enough: Take the time to read with your child.

What Sort of Reading Instruction Will Your Child Receive?

For almost a century, there has been debate in educational circles over the best way to teach reading. Currently, the two main methods, each with their ardent advocates, are:

- Phonics, which emphasizes the sounding out of syllables and the piecemeal decoding of words
- Whole language or Balanced Reading, which encourages children to use the knowledge they have of language and expression to draw meaning from texts.

Fortunately, you will not need to know where one ends and the other begins. The likelihood is that your child's teacher will utilize a combination of these two approaches. At NEA, we recommend a hybrid that includes the development of language and thinking skills as well as phonemic awareness, phonics, decoding, word recognition, comprehension, vocabulary, and a sense of the organization of stories, articles, and other forms of text.

The reality is that students enter first grade (the point where reading really starts in school) with a wide range of reading levels. Some children seem to have an almost instinctual ease with reading. For others, it requires painstaking work. Teachers recognize the need to differentiate and adjust.

Most schools employ, to some degree, basal readers issued by educational publishers. These have the virtue of developing reading skills sequentially so that your child, and his teacher, can get a sense of that progress being made. Basal readers have been criticized for dull texts and unimaginative use of language. Most teachers supplement these with other books and reading material.

There are some school practices that could conceivably cause your child problems. You should be concerned about:

- Inconsistent teacher approaches to reading methods, which can create discontinuity as your child moves from grade to grade
- Reading instruction conducted in groups that are too large to permit individualized attention
- Children forced to miss other subject areas when pulled out of class for remedial reading
- Large group pencil and paper tests for children under the age of nine

Reading instruction practices you would like to see include:

- Allowing students long uninterrupted periods of time for reading
- Integration of reading with writing and verbal discussion
- Programs and texts assigned according to your child's achievement level, not his grade level
- Assessments conducted in small groups that measure a broad range of literacy developments

Tuning in to Your Child's Reading

An alert and informed parent can serve as an indispensable early warning system.

To play that role, you will need to have some broad appreciation for what the standard achievement levels are for your child's grade. Your child's teacher can brief you on what signs to look for in assessing reading competence.

You know where your child is stumbling. You know if there's a pattern to his mistakes. You know if there are blind spots. You know if a seemingly "bad attitude" is camouflage for deeper complications.

If you suspect that your child has some fundamental reading problems, don't hesitate to act. You should promptly seek advice from the teacher and school specialists. If assessment testing is in order, this should be done as soon as possible (see Chapter 3).

If teachers and counselors minimize or dispute your concerns, listen patiently to what they have to say. It is entirely possible that, lacking their experience and expertise, you have jumped to a premature conclusion.

If you persist in believing that your child is experiencing unusual difficulty in reading, don't back off. Ask the teacher to pay special attention. Have the resource specialists take another look. Listen to the experts but listen also to your intuition. If you wind up being wrong in your fears, that's a mistake I am sure the school will forgive.

Although your child is learning to read at school, he should continue to be encouraged to read at home.

One of the most valuable contributions you can make is to find a steady diet of books that are appropriate to your child's reading level and will engage him. These books do not have to be particularly edifying. They do not need to challenge the far edge of his capability. They can be cartoon books, mystery books, sports books, or classics of literature. The point is to have them available and to get your child in the habit of turning to them for enjoyment.

How to find these books? Ask the teacher or school librarian. Speak with other parents. Browse the bookstores. There are even books recommending good books. And don't forget your public library, which can be a marvelous place to encourage reading.

Will the Classroom Teacher Be a Capable Reading Instructor?

At least through the fourth grade, reading instruction is a primary focus of teachers. Most have been specifically trained in how to teach reading, and how to identify and correct common reading problems. Most elementary school teachers are, in effect, reading specialists.

If you feel your child is not receiving enough individual attention, that is another matter. If that is the case, talk to the teacher to see what can be done. Some schools provide Saturday classes or outside programs for extra reading instruction. It may be there are exercises you can be doing at home, outside the normal homework, to supplement what you feel is missing.

If your child needs additional help from the fifth grade on, it will probably have to come from a resource specialist or tutor. The classrooms in those grades have already made the transition into the *reading to learn* phase.

But remember: regardless of your child's situation, **it is the school's job to teach your child how to read.** If necessary, you need to step in to make sure this happens.

Making Sense of Math

At times it can seem almost perverse. As math becomes by all accounts more essential in our increasingly technological world, math curriculum has come to be seen by many parents as more alien and impenetrable. There is probably no other aspect of your child's schooling more likely to leave at least one of you feeling befuddled.

But if you don't completely recognize the math in your child's homework, think about how the world has changed since your own school days.

The math looks different because the world is different. Advances in science, technology, information processing and communication, combined with the changing workplace, make it necessary for all students to understand more complex mathematical ideas. However, the advances make it possible to learn math in different engaging ways that address diverse learning styles. It's also important to know that mathematics can be represented numerically, symbolically, and graphically.

All this represents a shift from the past. Math instruction in many schools is in a state of flux. This is the result of several factors: competing theories about the goals of math education; revised state standards and differing interpretations of them; uncertainty about the role of calculators and technology in student learning; poor communication between the math establishment and parents.

You, of course, don't wish to become mired in long-standing theoretical disputes about pedagogy. All you want is to know enough about what's going on to be able to help your child. (And perhaps not embarrass yourself!)

What Are the Issues Underlying Math Education?

The teaching and learning of math has two central components that need not—but can—be in conflict with each other.

We want our children to learn **mathematical content**. Traditionally, this begins with arithmetic—the meaning and use of numbers. This "traditional" learning has historically involved repetitive drills and exercises using precisely delineated algorithms.

We also want our children to **understand** math processes

that define ways to reason, communicate, and make connections that help solve real world problems and achieve logical thinking. This comprehensive approach emphasizes the need for students to conceptualize math functions and be able to use them in real world problem-solving ways.

To do this, teachers try to strike an optimal blend between teaching the traditional "algorithms" of math (the procedures used to arrive at a correct answer) and root understandings of why those procedures work.

Ideally, your child should achieve a firm grasp of basic mathematical concepts along with a full appreciation of how math is more than a list of rules to be memorized. It is a tool for making sense of practical situations.

Complication can set in when schools, under pressure to show improvement on standardized test scores, take short-cuts that distort the role of rote drills.

Learning What Your Child Is Learning

Your worst apprehension is probably that you won't understand what your child is being taught, or that your child won't understand it.

Let me reassure you. For all the rhetoric about "new math," "whole math," or whatever other names you hear, the math instruction your child receives will likely be less confusing and more "normal" than you anticipate.

Yes, it probably differs from what you were taught, or what you recall of what your were taught. But core constructs are essentially unchanged.

If you find textbooks and worksheets baffling, it is probably for the same reasons that some students do—either the directions are not what you expected or you have not paid sufficient attention to what is being asked in the problem. When in doubt, ask. Teachers will be forthcoming and not mysterious about their goals and practices.

You can ask your child's teacher:

- To describe what math will be taught, and identify any methods that might logically strike you as new or unfamiliar
- To explain how this math might differ from "traditional" instruction
- To recommend ways (books, activities, websites) for you to stay apprised of what your child is learning
- What the proper role is for calculators in your child's work
- For suggestions on ways to identify ways to make the math your child is studying relevant to home situations

The nature of math instruction shifts, sometimes drastically, between lower and upper grades. Nonetheless, there are some elements you'd like to find in your child's classroom at every grade level:

- Math is used in various areas of study, not simply as a separate field. Efforts should be made to use math skills in history, science, health, art, geography, etc.
- Manipulatives such as blocks and rods are used, especially in the lower grades, as well as measuring devices like rulers and thermometers.
- A problem-solving approach is emphasized.
- Your child understands how she arrived at a correct answer and has an appreciation that there might be other ways to solve a problem correctly.
- Homework problems that apply math to real life situations are assigned.
- Efforts are made to give students confidence in their abilities to think in mathematical terms and concepts.

What You Can Do at Home to Help Your Child

In the same way you strive to create a home environment with reading as a centerpiece, so should you look for ways to bring math into your child's daily life.

Without a lot of strain, you can probably find many ways that math plays a role around the home. Remember that math is not just about counting; it involves pattern recognition, collecting and analyzing data, problem solving, and logically communicating an idea. From recipes in the kitchen to the budgeting for a shopping trip to the statistics on the sports page of the newspaper, your household offers many ways to bring numbers and their usefulness into your child's awareness. (Ask your child's teacher for ideas or search some of the websites listed at the end of the chapter.)

Remember that math will be crucial throughout your child's schooling. Your goal is to help her view math not as a chore, but as a challenge comparable in excitement to learning a musical instrument or a sport.

What About the Role of Calculators?

Studies show that calculators can be used to help children learn to understand math, and do not hurt a student's ability to perform calculations the traditional way, using paper and pencil.

With more frequency, calculators are being introduced into math classes, especially when your child's school adopts a standards-based curriculum. Using calculators is increasingly permitted on state and national assessment tests. However, their place in regular math curriculum varies from classroom to classroom, and district to district.

Teachers are sometimes cautious about introducing significant use of calculators for elementary math functions until a student has mastered those functions. A 1996 survey showed that less than one third of fourth graders used calculators at least once a week, while more than half of eighth graders were using them almost every day.

With homework, your child should probably not be using calculators on math problems until the teacher explicitly sanctions it.

The Big Picture

The areas discussed in this chapter—report cards, curriculum, reading and math instruction—may seem to you to be long-standing practices virtually set in stone. In point of fact, these practices are frequently reevaluated. As would be the case in the medical professions, teaching periodically adjusts itself to the emergence of new insights and new methods.

This reappraisal and revision of teaching and learning occurs as part of a constant interchange between academic theoreticians, educational administrators, and teachers seeking improved methods. The issues can become rather complex and arcane, and they can also become politically charged.

To teach the new math? To increase the number of report card categories? To emphasize whole language instruction? To switch the foreign language requirement? This can all seem a bit bewildering and even chaotic.

But remember that schools are, after all, living institutions constantly responding to a shifting environment. It would be as unhealthy for schools to refuse to change as it would be for them to constantly change. Somewhere in between is the right mix, and that's what we strive for.

WEBSITES

Math Help *www.figurethis.org*
America Reads *www.ed/gov/inits.americareads/kids.htm*
Kids Learning Network *www.KLNlive.com*

13

School Choice:
What Choice Do You Have?

In its most simple form, "choice" means allowing children to attend whatever public school they want, regardless of location. In other words, students can, if they wish, attend a public school that is not necessarily in their neighborhood.

The popular discussion of "choice" has increasingly centered on the controversial proposal known as "vouchers," and the entire concept of choice is frequently misconstrued to encompass vouchers alone. Before the highly politicized push for public vouchers, school choice was an option advocated mainly by educational reformers who believed it would help equalize opportunity between students who live in different neighborhoods, and equalize resources among the schools.

In point of fact, there are several different ways that school choice can be implemented. The ways in which this might occur fall into two basic categories:

- Intra-district choice, which allows students to attend schools within their home district. Many large cities, such as New York, Boston, Minneapolis, and Seattle use this.
- Interdistrict choice, which allows students to voluntarily attend schools in other districts in the state. Fourteen states, including Minnesota, Nebraska, and Wisconsin, use this, and many others states are considering it.

There are several forms of choice-type schools:

223

- **magnet** schools, which often focus on a specialty or method (technology, Montessori)
- **charter** schools, which are publicly funded but run independently, often with a focus on a teaching philosophy or an emphasis on community
- **vouchers,** where students attend private schools with their tuition provided by public funds. (The constitutionality of vouchers is being challenged in court.)

Do You Have a Choice?

Not all school districts do.

Asking at the school superintendent's office is the easiest way to determine what, if any, choice you have concerning which public school your child can attend. As has been mentioned elsewhere, conferring with other savvy parents is always an excellent way to learn about your options.

Public choice students currently comprise some 14 percent of overall K–12 enrollment, many of these in large cities that offer intradistrict options. Some 300,000 students nationwide are now crossing to schools outside their district. (Many are special education students traveling to where more appropriate services are offered.)

Some eighteen states currently have laws permitting some form of school choice. At least thirty-six states have charter school legislation. It should not be difficult for you to discover if you have any choice about which public school your child can attend.

One of the biggest practical obstacles to exercising your right to choice is that families often must provide transportation. For this and other reasons, choice has not always been as attractive to parents as planners anticipated.

Charter Schools

Charter schools come in many shapes and forms, and the laws governing what they can and cannot be vary from state to state.

There are really only two commonalities: 1) charter schools are public schools, in that they receive public funding; 2) they have been freed of some of the regulations that apply to other public schools.

Many charter schools tend to be smaller than regular public schools and place an emphasis on involving parents and teachers to a greater degree. They hire their own teachers and can create their own curriculum as well as teaching methods. The three most common reasons cited for creating a charter school are:

- To realize an educational vision
- To serve a special population
- To be free from many bureaucratic restrictions

The NEA, which sponsors several charter schools, believes that every sound charter school should feature:

- Open admission
- Parents and staff who are involved in the design and governance of the school
- Teachers who are certified professionals
- Compliance with the same fiscal and academic accountability that applies to any public school

Charter schools have been in existence for the past ten years. Some thirty-seven states have laws permitting charter schools. In school year 2000–2001, charter schools served more than 500,000 students. The highest concentrations of charter schools are in Arizona, California, Florida, Michigan and Texas.

Controversy has often surrounded charter schools due to the politicized agenda of some of the concept's advocates. Conservative, free-market proponents view charter schools as a means of "competing" with local public schools in a way they hope might eventually challenge the centralized educational establishment.

Conversely, other charter school advocates are progressive reformers who see in them opportunities for educational innovation, teacher empowerment, and heightened responsiveness to diverse and minority populations.

There is no question that the charter school movement has considerable momentum as well as deep bipartisan support in the political arena.

Still, it is possible for your child to proceed through her entire school career without charter schools being even a remote consideration. They may not be located nearby to where you live (a good possibility) or you will be satisfied with your local school and have no interest in experimentation.

But for more and more families, charter schools are emerging, depending on circumstances, as an option to consider.

Who Can Apply?

Charter schools are public schools and there is no restriction on who can apply.

High enrollment is essential for charter schools. They must attract their own students and retain them. As a result, if and when one gets established in your area, you are likely to hear about it. They advertise. They promote. They vigorously spread the word.

Some schools are quite popular, and are in the position of turning down applicants. Admission procedures vary greatly, and you will have to check with the school to learn the details regarding entrance exams and applying.

Tuition at Charter Schools

Charter schools are free, just like any public school.

There may be some extra costs involved in sending your child to a charter school, principally regarding transportation, uniforms, or supplies. Since finding suitable space is sometimes a problem, charter schools can locate, or relocate, to a place of lesser geographical convenience. Getting your child to school and back is your responsibility.

As largely start-up ventures, sometimes with marginal funding, charter schools frequently stage a variety of fund-raising activities which can be directed at parents. These are not (and legally cannot be) in the form of an assessment.

Will Your Role as Parent Be Different in a Charter School?

Many charter schools are started explicitly with a family/community model in mind, wherein parents are considered integral to the operation and success of the school. Parents who send their children to a charter school often do so out of a clear desire to be more actively involved. In addition, some charter schools ask parents to sign a contract affirming their involvement with their child's schooling.

(As noted elsewhere in this book, regular public schools have no shortage of needs for your participation, and you, on behalf of your child, have abundant reasons—if not always time—to be maximally involved.)

Thus, if your child is enrolled in a charter school, you will, from the beginning, be confronted with an intensified set of expectations for your role. Charter school parents are often asked to assist in the classroom as aides, and to contribute to the physical work of maintaining or renovating the facility.

The most significant difference between regular public schools and charter schools is governance. Many of the legal charters authorizing the establishment of the schools require parental participation on the school's governing board.

Evaluating a Charter School

Since many charter schools are quite new, it is sometimes difficult to receive the type of concrete reassurance concerning quality—testimony of graduates, test scores, performance of graduates at the higher educational levels—that you might want.

That shouldn't prevent you from reviewing the information that is, or should be, available, such as:

- What percentage of the teachers are certified?
- How many years of experience do the teachers have?
- What sort of extracurricular activities are offered?
- What is the average class size?
- Does the school have a specialty or focus?
- What is the rate of entering students who (so far) stay on until graduation?
- What is the financial stability of the school?

It has recently come to light that many states have neglected, partly due to the vagueness of the statutes, to hold some charter schools to one of the key elements of their charter: the need to demonstrate academic improvement by students.

In coming years, the monitoring of charter schools will be tightened up, most likely in the form of rigorously measuring aggregate test scores. As noted in Chapter 7, this can be a questionable means of rating a school.

A Few Words on Vouchers

Vouchers—a program for sending children whose parents are dissatisfied with the local public school to a private school of their "choice," with the state paying for tuition—continues to be a proposal that receives ardent support from certain sectors of the ideological right and elsewhere.

As a practical matter, vouchers have their greatest appeal to inner city residents whose schools are often in deplorable condition. Middle-class families are more content with their schools and already have choice: They can often afford to send their children to private school if need be. The fact is that under a voucher system, public funds would be diverted to many families who already send their children to private schools but pay their own way.

Furthermore, as Richard Kahlenberg points out in his book, *All Together Now: Creating Middle-Class Schools Through Public School Choice*, "Research suggests that most choice schemes that include private schools will exacerbate socioeconomic concentrations, rather than alleviate them, by skimming off the best and most motivated students . . . greater segregation is likely to result."

Unlike public schools, private schools are not required to accept all children. In fact, some parochial schools reject as many as two-thirds of the applicants. The likelihood is that private schools will choose precisely those students that any school would, the best and the brightest.

What happens to those children not accepted? You don't hear much about that. The great fallacy of vouchers is that they pretend to be a marketplace solution mostly for impoverished communities that long ago were abandoned by the mainstream marketplace. I find that sad and, frankly, deceitful.

For me, the voucher question is ultimately one of how we spend public money on education. Do we invest in public schools, in proven reforms like reduced class size and increased teacher training, or do we spend it on an experiment that at best may serve only a few?

The Big Picture

The overwhelming first choice for most parents is the one they already have: a quality local public school. Where interdistrict choice exists, in states like Wisconsin and Minnesota, surprisingly few families avail themselves of it.

And for reasons that make sense. Geographic convenience is no small thing to a child or parent. Another reason, one that gets conveniently overlooked by the ideological sabre-rattlers, is that the community school, as much as any institution in this country, is the place where families join with other families in a full commitment to create the best opportunities for their children and the children of fellow citizens. It's called working together, and it is basic to the American spirit.

Yes, choice has its place in encouraging innovation and empowering families. But if quality education is ultimately what parents seek, why overlook the obvious? We know what works. Smaller classes. Skilled teachers provided with quality professional development opportunities. Up-to-date textbooks and equipment. Programs in place to help all children succeed. Facilities in good repair. Parental involvement. Open communication. Shared commitment to high standards.

In the exciting clamor over enhancing our "choice," I think it's useful to remember that making your local school the best it can be will quite probably be your first choice.

14

More Resources That Can Help Your Child

Schools increasingly recognize that they need to provide diverse types of assistance to students and families. Since at some point in your child's schooling you'll have reason to use some of these services, it helps to know in advance what's available.

Making Use of the School Staff

In addition to the teachers and front office administrators, public schools employ either directly in the school or share on a district-wide basis several types of professionals who may prove quite useful over the course of your child's schooling. These include the school psychologist, the school nurse, and resource specialists (special ed, speech and hearing, reading).

Although none of these may be as essential as the primary classroom teacher, they all contribute, often significantly, to your child's schooling. The school office or your child's teacher can identify who these people are, what their responsibilities are, and how you or your child can arrange to see them.

School Psychologist

Unlike the stereotype of an adult's relationship to a psychologist (one-on-one sessions exclusively focusing on emotional and psychological issues), the public school psychologist's primary function is usually to identify and assess your child's school-related problems.

"We're known primarily as the assessors," says Lori Shnider Glassman, president of the Florida Association of School Psychologists. "Dealing with a child's emotions is only a small piece of what we do."

The school psychologist is someone who understands school systems and the complications that can arise from a child's interaction with them. As a resource, psychologists provide a supplement to teachers, families and administrators in solving a range of school problems.

What are the main responsibilities of the school psychologist?

Assessment services. Referred by the teacher, parent, or staff, the psychologist becomes involved in determining the needs of the child and the most promising remedies. If these remedies fail, the psychologist refers the child for further evaluation.

Consultation. The psychologist works with parent, teacher, and the child team to create strategies for helping the child with a range of school-related difficulties, from motivation to oppositional behavior.

Counseling. The psychologist runs groups to help children with certain difficulties, like AD/HD or problems related to divorce and other social issues.

Crisis Response. The psychologist is often pivotal in the school's planning for and response to traumatic events, like incidents of violence or other tragedies.

Testing. The psychologist will be the one to administer or direct individualized assessment testing of a child, and often will be called on by schools to evaluate performance on state or national tests.

If your child is referred to the school psychologist, regardless of the reason, the school is obligated to notify you. Before the psychologist can work with your child, you must give your written consent.

If you feel your child could benefit from seeing the psychologist, you can initiate the meeting.

Most schools share a psychologist with one or more schools

in the district. The National Association of School Psychologists recommends a student to psychologist ratio of 1000–1; many districts exceed that, and some by a far margin. Obviously, psychologists not overburdened by their case load will have more time for standard forms of counseling.

School psychologists have specialized training in both psychology and education. Most states currently require new hires to have an educational specialist degree, whereas a master's in school psychology has previously been the norm.

School Nurse

Chances are that your school either has a nurse on the premises or has one available throughout the district on a floating basis. The nurse's role is an evolving one.

The traditional function of tending to sore throats and bruises resulting from recess mishaps still applies. Also, the nurse is in charge of the various screenings (hearing, eyesight, respiratory ailments, etc.) that are required of public schools by state law. And the nurse is primarily responsible for overseeing the welfare of students with special health-related needs.

If your child suffers from a health condition or chronic disease such as diabetes or asthma, it's a good idea to communicate directly with the nurse (in addition to filling out the normal health forms at the start of the school year). This is especially true if your child requires medication during the course of the school day.

By meeting with the nurse, you'll be able to talk through any contingencies the school should be aware of and ways that the staff can be enlisted to help.

In addition to these responsibilities, the nurse can also be called on, depending on her expertise and the responsiveness of the administration, to perform such functions as:

- Acting as a resource for classroom health education
- Serving on the child study team

- Monitoring the environmental health of the school (safety of the playground equipment, allergic reactions to building features)
- Administering prescribed medication to students
- Serving on the school's crisis management team

Optimally, says Dr. Judy Robinson, executive director of the National Association of School Nurses, "the nurse should function as the health official for the school."

Resource and Curriculum Specialists

School districts often employ specialists with focused expertise in certain academic areas. These specialists can be located full-time at the school, but more often they will split their time among various schools within a district. These specialists serve in several capacities: diagnosing and helping students who are having difficulty; assisting teachers with strategies to help these students; advising administrators on ways of adapting to new state standards.

There are several reasons to know about these. Your child may be referred to a specialist and it's useful to know who that is, what their responsibilities are, and how they can be contacted. These specialists are often mainstays of the child study team and the Individual Education Plan (IEP) committee. Also, since they deal with students at different grade levels and in different classrooms, they are often well known like few other staff members throughout the entire school.

The specialists found most commonly in public schools are in the fields of:

Speech and language. Difficulties in speech and language need to be accurately assessed, and corrective measures taken as soon as possible.

Schools are your ally in this. They are required to provide help for any child with documented deficiencies. Your child can be referred to the speech and language pathologist either by teachers or by you. The main reasons for such referrals are concerns about articulation, fluency, decoding and other language skills.

You will be notified if your child has been referred for speech and language evaluation or therapy. The pathologist may see your child either singly or in a group, usually at least twice per week. Average sessions are twenty to thirty minutes long.

You ought to be kept apprised of what is being done with your child and the progress he is making. When children are pulled out of class for a session with the speech pathologist, efforts are generally made to minimize interference with classroom instruction. If you believe that is not the case, you should bring it to the attention of the teacher.

It's useful for you to speak directly with the pathologist, who ought to make herself available. Depending on your child's difficulty, this could be a brief, short-lived activity or an ongoing aspect of your child's school life. Also, it is common for the pathologist to recommend helpful exercises that you can practice with your child at home.

Reading. Most elementary school teachers are, in effect, reading experts. Nonetheless, many schools and school districts feature a reading specialist trained to perform several important functions. Reading specialists can do in-depth diagnostic screening of students having reading difficulties and may have the time, which the classroom teacher may not, for working individually with the student or in small groups.

Additionally, the reading specialist will work with teachers, offering instructions in different techniques for teaching reading, helping them plan their reading exercises, and arranging tutors for certain students.

Special education. Schools routinely provide the services of one or more special education counselors, who can both teach those students who qualify for their services or assist regular teachers who have special ed students included in their classroom. In addition, the special education resource person will often participate on the child study team.

Alternative Education

More and more school districts now offer so-called alternative education, which is an innovative way of addressing the problems of students whose emotional or behavioral problems make the normal classroom situation difficult. Once limited mainly to high schools, there are an increasing number of such programs available both at the middle and elementary school levels.

(Note: These programs should not be confused with efforts to create differently structured experimental curriculum, although such programs share the name "alternative" and may occupy a similar role as an adjunct to normal school.)

Alternative schools are designed for students who are academically capable but either completely fail to perform or by their disruptions prevent other students from performing. Some are severe troublemakers on the brink of expulsion, while others can be habitually anti-authoritarian or truants.

The key feature is a low student-teacher ratio and a special effort to infuse curriculum with a system of emotional support and instruction in social skills. "One of the main ingredients is simply size," explains Dr. Norman Zamcheck, who supervises alternative ed programs in Norwalk, Connecticut. "Kids get the opportunity to work closely with teachers and aides who know their strengths and can help them overcome their weaknesses."

Alternative programs can be located in a classroom, an adjoining trailer, or a wing of an existing school, but the students in these programs are generally kept separate from the regular school population. Sometimes the alternative ed program has its own building.

A student is generally "nominated" for alternative education by teachers and staff. The time a student spends in alternative ed varies, but most programs try to set time parameters, with a minimum stay (usually one year) and a maximum (perhaps eighteen months). The process of returning to the normal classroom (which is the goal of most programs) should be closely monitored to make sure that the student successfully makes the transition.

After-School Programs

"After-school" or "extended day" programs are an important service that more and more public schools provide. If your school does not offer such a program, it will likely have some affiliation (lending its facilities, providing transportation to another location, etc.) with a local service agency that does.

These after-school programs are particularly useful for families with working parents who are unable or unwilling to leave children home alone or with another trusted adult. But after-school programs are also valuable for children who need the added companionship, stimulation and, yes, study time.

As schools clamor to meet these expanding needs, they must also grapple with shifting concepts of what these programs should be about.

Should the emphasis be on fun, with sports and crafts and games? Should it resemble a continuation of school, with tutors and projects? Should it be structured? Unstructured? Rigorous? Relaxed?

Do you know which your child prefers? Which you want for your child? And which is best for her?

What Are These Programs Like?

They go by different names: after-school; out-of-school, extended day; school-age child care; expanded learning; etc.

And the array of names only begins to suggest the array of services these programs can offer. Basically, they attempt to serve, either singly or in some combination, three objectives:

1. Child care, with an emphasis on supervision of children of working families
2. Extended learning, with a focus on academic enrichment and using this extra time to make up for gaps in a child's achievement

3. Youth development, with the goal of promoting positive activities and preventing risky behavior

Striking the right balance between these different goals is not easy. Accordingly, there is great variation in how programs structure themselves.

What's offered can include:

- Homework help and tutoring
- Study time, hopefully in a quiet environment
- Enrichment activities such as field trips, group learning projects, educational movies, etc.
- Performing arts such as music and drama that have been dropped from the normal school day, as well as visual arts, cooking, etc.
- Recreation—your basic recess—following the long school day

The recent boom in interest in after-school programs is largely driven by escalating pressures on student achievement and the need for outside-the-home child care. Program directors are ever mindful of the need to create a satisfying experience for students. After-school programs generally make an effort to cater to the interests of the children (which, of course, can take dozens of forms on any given day). As Ellen Gannett, co-director of the National Institute for Out-of-School-Time, observes, "It's hard to force them to go. The kids vote with their feet."

Assessing the Quality of a Program

By far the best way to decide if this is a good fit for your child— and a safe one—is to visit and see for yourself. Speak with the director and staff. You should also try to speak with parents who have children currently enrolled. If you don't know anyone, the program director should be willing to supply some references.

Several criteria are important for a sound program:

- Adequately trained and decently paid personnel. (There is a great variety in who's hired—and who these programs are able to hire.)
- Group size, staff ratio. (Optimally, there should be no more than twenty-five to thirty students in a group, and the staff–student ratio should be no greater than one to thirteen, according to Ellen Gannett.)
- Good facilities, with enough space to allow both quiet activities and active play
- Flexible structure and a choice of activities. (Following the rigors of a normal school day, this is particularly important. Your child's wants and needs will vary from day to day. What you want for your child may shift throughout the year.)
- Varied programs that can accommodate age ranges and various types of activities (not just day care for youngsters)
- Ample and varied materials for play and for study
- Decent snacks
- A learning atmosphere (quiet space, desks)
- Safe playground and facility

How Much Will This Cost?

Due to grants and other subsidies, some schools are able to provide after-school activities free of charge. Others operate on a fee basis that can cost as much as several hundred dollars per month.

The Big Picture

As our society continues to undergo transformations both large and small, we continue to look to the public school for solutions. I can't help but notice that for all the problems and complaints about public schools, people are clamoring for schools to take on ever greater responsibilities and to serve children in more varied ways.

I think I know why that is, and it's not because schools are as lavishly funded and as tightly run as any for-profit business. It's because the people in need, children and parents, generally trust that the school will care. That says a lot.

15

"EduSpeak" Terms to Know

Nothing puts you at a disadvantage quite so much as not knowing what the teacher, principal, or resource specialist is talking about when they casually employ a terminology or phrase that you simply do not understand. Suddenly, you are no better than the second grader in the back of the class, not sure if you should interrupt to ask what the term means or continue on in the hope that the unfolding context will sooner or later make it intelligible to you.

As I've mentioned, schools can become, without intending so, insular worlds that don't always take the time to acknowledge the world beyond its walls. Nowhere is this as evident as it is in the vocabulary that is routinely used by school staff. Many of the phrases which may strike you as defiantly obscure are part of the normal daily dialogue that goes on among education professionals.

No doubt they could do a better job of translating their lingo for your benefit. And many, in fact, do so. But just in case they don't, and just in case you're the type who is too shy or proud to raise your hand and ask what the heck *that* means, I offer the following glossary of frequently used EduSpeak terms.

Ability or **aptitude tests** are designed to measure what a student is capable of and what is that student's capacity for learning. I.Q. tests are the best known of the ability tests.

Achievement tests are those tests which measure how much a student has learned in certain subject areas. They are to be distinguished from ability tests. The high-stakes standardized tests

241

increasingly used by states to evaluate school performance are achievement tests.

Alternative schools, at least as the phrase is used in the context of public schools, refers to special schools or programs designed to meet the needs of a distinct population, usually students who are having difficulty with regular schools.

Assessment refers to an effort, by the teacher, specialist, counselor, or school, to determine the level of learning a student has achieved. There are various forms of assessment instruments, including tests, portfolios, and performance.

At-risk refers to students who have a high risk of failing or dropping out of school. The term often has implicit sociological implications, and can refer to children from underprivileged or problem-ridden home situations.

Basal reader is the type of textbook and literature collection that is used to teach beginning readers. They are created explicitly for use in reading instruction in the early grades.

Charter schools differ widely but have two main features in common: They are public schools, in that they receive public funding and they have been freed of some of the statutes that apply to other public schools so long as they produce positive academic results within a stated period of time. Many charter schools tend to be smaller than regular public schools and place an emphasis on involving parents and teachers to a greater degree. They hire their own teachers and can create their own curriculum as well as teaching methods.

Cooperative learning is a teaching strategy that emphasizes students working together in a small team situation to solve problems. The idea is to better instruct children in some of the techniques—sharing information, adapting to the abilities of others, etc.—that are important in nonacademic situations.

Curriculum refers either to all the courses taught at a school or the courses offered in a certain field, like math or social studies.

The curriculum is commonly a written plan stipulating what students will be taught.

Differentiated instruction is teaching that attempts to take into consideration various learning styles and achievement levels of individual students, rather than rely on a one-size-fits-all approach.

Enrichment is a term used for activities and subjects that are outside the routine of the regular classroom but are beneficial. "Enrichment programs" are those that supplement what a child is learning in the classroom, or take that learning to a higher level. Enrichment options are frequently used both for gifted and at-risk learners.

Gifted and talented are terms ascribed to students of exceptional ability. It is meant to apply to students who are not just smart, but *very smart*. Many schools try to establish separate programs for these children, realizing that a regular classroom may leave them, at least in some subject areas, significantly underchallenged.

Heterogeneous grouping is the practice of grouping students of varying skills and abilities together in a classroom or small group situation. The opposite, grouping students together of like skills and abilities, is termed homogeneous grouping.

Immersion usually refers to an intensive means of teaching a second language wherein the student is "immersed" in a classroom that functions very much bilingually. Many immersion programs are for students from foreign language backgrounds, with English being the language they are being immersed in.

Inclusion is the practice of including, to the maximum extent possible, children with disabilities in regular classrooms. The terms by which this practice is legally mandated are set forth in the federal Individual with Disabilities Education Act (IDEA).

Individual Education Plan (IEP) amounts to an intervention strategy. Used mostly, but not exclusively, for special needs children, it represents a guideline of strategies and goals to be followed for the school year. Formulated by a committee that includes teachers, resource counselors, and the child's parent or guardian, the IEP represents the school's best assessment concerning the nature of your child's difficulties and what approaches hold the most promise. It is a written, legal contract stipulating services the school will provide.

Invented spelling is a technique, coupled with phonemic awareness, for encouraging children to practice writing without becoming intimidated by the need for correct spelling. It can sometimes be a shock for new parents to see their child praised for writing strewn with wrongly spelled (but nonetheless intelligible) words, but that's invented spelling.

Learning disability is a condition that, simply put, makes it difficult for a student to learn. The cause of this can range from physiological (sub-par hearing and vision) to cognitive (deficient math processing) to emotional. Dyslexia is the most common, and best known example of a learning disability.

Learning style or **learning difference** is a concept that recognizes the recent developments in neuroscience and cognitive theory pointing to the many different ways by which children learn. This concept increasingly informs the practice of teaching, especially with slow or underachieving students.

Looping is the practice of having an entire class continue with the same teacher for more than one school year.

Magnet schools are public schools often distinguished by a more focused type of education. Magnet schools tend to feature a particular specialty (technology) or teaching philosophy (Montessori). Students must apply for admission. They are considered alternatives to regular public schools.

Mainstreaming is the practice of including students with learning or others types of disabilities into regular classrooms.

Manipulatives are learning materials that students touch and handle as a way of facilitating their learning. These are widely used in the lower primary grades, especially for math, and also used where possible with children whose learning difference suggests a preference for tactile modes of learning.

Outcomes are the results of the teaching and learning that takes place at the school. It is a phrase used by educators as a synonym for goals.

Phonics refers to the basic relationships between letters and sounds. It is an elementary method of teaching reading. *Sounding out the word* is the operative element of phonics teaching.

Portfolio is the collection of your child's work—tests, writing exercises, artwork, reports, etc.—that the teacher maintains as a record of your child's learning. A way you may encounter the term is "portfolio assessment," which is to say an evaluation of your child on the basis of his total classroom output rather than a test result.

Remedial education or **remediation** refers to teaching effort specifically geared to helping students catch up with their peers.

Resource room is a designated space (sometimes more than one room) where students go for special help, which can range from special education classes to small group or one-on-one instruction in special needs like speech and reading.

School choice is a term which formerly meant having the option to attend public schools other than the one assigned on a neighborhood-basis. Choice, in recent years, has been the name used by advocates for vouchers, which is the practice of allowing parents dissatisfied with the local public school to send their children to a private school of their "choice."

Special needs students refers to children who require special education due to physical, cognitive, emotional or other types of disabilities.

Standards are, at least in their most common current usage, guidelines for what students should know and be able to do at certain grade levels. You are most likely to come across this term in the context of how schools are shaping curriculum to state standards, which are being developed and revised in response to social and political pressures.

Team teaching is a technique whereby two or more teachers work jointly with a group of students.

Tracking is the practice of aggregating students according to their perceived abilities. The practice has been reduced or eliminated in some elementary schools, at least in its overt form. It exists in middle schools in various ways and more so in high schools.

Vouchers is the practice of allowing parents dissatisfied with the local public school to send their children to a private school of their "choice," with tuition paid for through a voucher. The legality of this is currently being challenged in state and federal courts.

Whole language is a teaching strategy that emphasizes reading for overall meaning and content (the "wholeness" of words and texts), forgiving specific mistakes in misreading or mispronouncing words and phrases. In this sense, it is a companion technique to invented spelling.

16

Parent Involvement from A to Z

I preach parent involvement because it is *guaranteed*—as few things are—to produce positive results. And I preach it with a special poignancy because I wish I had been more involved with my daughters' schooling.

Yes, I was one of those parents who was very, very busy. Because my job was in the field of education I could argue (to myself) that in some vague way my work constituted my involvement. I could argue (to myself) that my work would not get done if I diminished my commitment to it by spending more time with my children's school. I didn't dispute that my involvement was needed—by my daughters or their school; I simply argued (to myself) that my time was more importantly spent at my job.

I would do it differently if I had it to do over again, and I hope you won't look back with the same regret.

Guilt, I have learned, is an unreliable way to motivate anyone to do anything. And if you're like most parents, you have plenty of that already. To be involved, you have to *want to be involved*. And the only way that will occur is if you have compelling, meaningful, personal incentives for doing so.

There are plenty of them out there.

Start with the most basic incentive of all: to show your child with action, not just words, that you really care about education. I cannot overstate the value to your child of seeing that your involvement with school extends beyond simply getting her to the bus on time.

There is also what I might call a preventive reason for you to be involved. The more familiar you are with the workings of the school and the more the school knows about you, the better off your child will be. As Veronica Fowler, an Ames, Iowa, parent commented, "Sooner or later you're going to need to deal with the school on your child's behalf. You're in a much better position if that's not the first time they've seen you."

In addition, schools depend on your support. There are numerous important tasks where parent volunteers are critical. In this case, the old adage applies: If you're not part of the solution, you're part of the problem.

Finally, involvement is a fabulous—one time only!—chance for you to learn invaluable lessons about your child, about the inner life of the school, and, frankly, about yourself.

All pretty good reasons, if you ask me. As Dr. Seuss' *Cat in the Hat* says, "There's work to be done."

Options for Getting Involved

Involvement in your child's schooling, like involvement in the political arena, begins close to home and, depending on your time and appetite and need, expands outward to encompass broader concerns. Here are some ways you can contribute.

Helping Your Child at Home

The evidence is clear. Your child's chances for success in school are immeasurably enhanced by your direct involvement. Some at-home habits to pay attention to are:

Reading. Studies have shown that nothing strengthens a child's academic progress like being read to at home and having a home environment that values reading.

Motivation. It's essential for your child to know that *you* value learning. Look for ways to demonstrate how learning has helped, could help, or is helping you. Remember to acknowledge effort as well as success in appraising your child's school work.

Study. Regular times for doing homework, a reasonably quiet spot to do it in, and proximity to you or another adult are helpful elements. In interacting with your child over homework, look for ways to encourage not just completion of the assignment but "understanding" of it.

Thinking skills. Listen closely to your child's conversation and try to draw it into areas of learning. Encourage your child to ask questions, reward curiosity. If you lack answers (hey, it can happen to the best of us) here's your chance to model ways to research information.

Helping the Teacher

Even if I were not the president of the nation's largest teacher organization, I would point out that teachers are frequently overwhelmed with busy work which in any other profession would be performed by a team of assistants. Time spent on busy work is often time subtracted from more important tasks, in this case your child's education.

Almost all teachers need help. But not all teachers ask for it, or know how to ask for it. Some teachers may send notes home in your child's backpack or folder announcing when they have an acute need, such as old sponges for a science project and two parents to help out with it. Others elect to do the work all by themselves. My advice is to ask the teacher at the start of the year where they are likely to need help, and to ask again periodically. Don't be shy or worry about seeming to be pushy. If you're not needed, teachers will let you know.

Among the areas where you can be useful are:

In-class assistance. There are various ways that you can work directly with the children, from reading them stories to playing educational games to monitoring messy science and art projects. Helping out with such group activities can be particularly valuable to a teacher seeking some one-on-one time with his students. As the teacher discovers what you are adept at doing, classroom time may be adjusted to make better use of your skills. If you are uncomfortable with any part of your role, talk it through with the teacher.

Material support. Inventive teachers seeking ways to make lessons more lively will often use a rich assortment of materials—pipe cleaners, plastic bowls, bags of flour, wrapping paper, mounds of play dough. When the school budget does not provide these, as is often the case, teachers can either purchase the materials themselves, which many do at a considerable cost of time and money, or rely on parent contributions.

Administrative work. From compiling attendance records to filing instructional forms, teachers have numerous clerical responsibilities that they may be delighted to delegate to a parent volunteer. Many schools try to establish a system of "room parents" who can act as a liaison both for the coordination of volunteer help and for emergency events like school closings due to weather. Otherwise, these labor intensive chores fall—you guessed it—to the teacher.

Field trips and enrichment activities. Chaperones are needed, and often required, for field trips to museums, historical landmarks, and other supplemental learning venues.

Helping the School

Many parents are quite surprised to discover that schools, for all their vaunted bureaucracy, are often extremely accessible and open to outside input. It is not entirely to a school's credit that this fact should be verging on a secret. It's fine that your school appreciates your participation, but it also needs to find ways for actively soliciting and promoting it.

Places where you can probably be of use to your school are:

Library or media center. Whereas the school may have a paid professional staff person in charge of this facility on a full- or part-time basis, there is always a need for more help. This can take the form of simple shelving of books, assisting students and parents looking for suitable books, and serving as a resource for students engaged in research projects. Parents with computer skills are always needed to guide students in software programs or to untangle technology-related complications.

Communications. Regular newsletters and issue-specific memorandum are vital elements of a school's relationship to its community. Such communications can make all the difference between a school that generates enthusiastic support and one that keeps parents at arm's length. Parents, in coordination with the principal's office, are often responsible for most, if not all, of the writing and production of these.

In addition, more ambitious parent groups have developed their own newsletters, separate from the school, to express opinions and rally support for various projects.

Schools are an easy target for those politicians and pundits and local gossips who often have little interest in the facts of the matter. Thus, schools have an ongoing need for public relations and publicity, only some of which they are equipped to perform on their own. Let's face it; public schools often receive a bad rap that is far from justified.

"You'd go to the park up the street, and parents would be saying all these terrible things about the local school," recalls Sandra Halladey, a San Francisco parent who at the time was exploring kindergarten placement for her preschool daughter. "I looked into it and it's just not true." (Halladey, as a result of this experience, has gone on to become a local Parents for Public Schools activist.)

What are your school's good features? What positive attributes are little known or underappreciated? Notable student and faculty achievements (or even not so notable ones) can't find their way into local newspapers or onto television shows without press releases and direct overtures.

After-school clubs. Math club, chess club, science club, drama club are some examples of valuable after-school enrichment programs that often only exist with the dedication of parent volunteers. These are of particular value as schools are forced to concentrate their classroom focus to subjects that relate to standardized tests.

If you have a background in an area that can provide an enjoyable supplement to curriculum (or have the determination to go out and learn it anew), you might consider helping in this way. Schools vary in their guidelines for such clubs, so you will need to check with the school administration or veteran parents.

Remember that you do not need to take on this task by yourself. It's usually best to find a few other parents who share your interest and can share the work load.

Fund-raising. This is probably the form of parent volunteerism that you're most familiar with—the bake sales, book sales, magazine drives, etc. I won't reiterate the details except to state the obvious: They do generate much-needed supplemental funds, often for special projects, at a time of budget squeeze; and they depend completely on parent involvement.

Soliciting and coordinating contributions from local businesses has become a promising aspect of school fund-raising. In recent years, the business community has begun to accept a larger responsibility. This has taken such forms as providing flex time so employees can mentor students to donating computers and technical expertise. Exciting possibilities remain to be developed in this area. With the increasing conviction that our economic future relies on an educated population, the time may be ripe for schools to pursue strong commitments from the business community.

Governance. Schools are not exactly democracies, but there are committees where decisions get made with binding consequences. Known variously as site councils or school councils, these committees can make crucial decisions on everything from budget allocations to the hiring of principals and teachers. Usually comprised of the principal and several teachers, these committees often require the participation of one or two parents. This is a classic way to make a difference in how your child's school is run, and who is running it.

Helping the Community

As I mentioned in the introduction to this book, being a public school parent is like joining a large club. You are part of a community that is not only the beneficiary of what the school provides but has direct influence over its ways and means.

Your city or town's school board is an obvious place to get involved. Running for office might be more than you want to sign up for, but helping out a candidate you approve of is a way of contributing. In many places, elections for the school board are hotly contested between public school advocates and critics. The makeup of the school board governs everything from the hiring of a superintendent to tough choices about which school programs to fund and which to discontinue.

Public policy issues that impact schools, such as tax increases and bond proposals, are subject to the mechanisms of political campaigns. Debate, issue formulation, and voter turn-out play an important role in determining which position wins or loses. As there would be in any electoral campaign, your participation here could make a difference.

Helping Yourself

If you're not aware of it already, schools are often wondrous and inspiring places. There is a palpable joy to being in them, around them, or working on behalf of them. In the period following last September's terrorist attacks, I found myself visiting, as part of my duties as NEA president, numerous public schools. In those grim days and weeks, I felt fortunate to meander along school corridors, peek into the classrooms, observe the timeless processes of teaching and learning.

Schools are, to a degree, sanctuaries from the urgent problems of the world. The business of schools is building for the future. In that respect, they are almost a refuge, places where the healing of the world can be done—if it can be done at all.

You may find, as I so often do, that there is something immensely replenishing in being at your child's school. As Kate Whittley, a Cupertino, California, parent and school volunteer, said, "You always take out more than you put in. You arrive at the school with a full bucket thinking you'll empty it out, and you return home with it overflowing."

Are There Issues Where You Can Make a Difference?

There are, in my opinion, a number of public policy issues in which parents should be far more influential than they have been. In this respect, public school parents are not unlike citizens throughout our democracy. The low percentage of voters who cast their vote and who actively participate in the political process falls far short of ideal.

Yet the reasons commonly offered for voter apathy, namely detachment from the political process and vagueness concerning the effect of the process on your life, ought not, it seems to me, apply to school-related issues. For when it comes to schools, there is no mystery how the issues affect your life. And, when it comes to the passionate determination you have to make sure your child enjoys a fine education, detachment from the process would hardly seem to be a factor.

What's needed is clear recognition that there are issues relevant to your child's schooling where you can have a greater impact. Here are some areas:

School quality. Every school district regularly engages in a debate over which school programs to emphasize, which to expand, which to diminish and which to drop. The same is true for such vital school quality issues as the pay structure for teachers and administrators, and funding for facilities maintenance and renovation. These debates are where community values come into play. The pros and cons of proposals are thrashed out in school site-councils, in superintendent's offices, and at the school board.

Is your voice, and that of like-minded parents, being heard?

School budget. Money is not the sole factor determining the fortune of public schools. But it is simply dishonest to speak of school improvement and reform without fully acknowledging the overwhelming importance of funding.

Furthermore, school funding frequently comes before voters in the form of special tax levies dedicated to school projects and budget referendums put forward by citizen groups and other organized constituents. The consequence of these cannot be overstated. The funding of schools is a contentious discussion in almost every town and city in the country. You can usually learn the details of the issues and proposals directly from your school board or from reliable local news outlets.

The political representatives who make ultimate decisions, as well as the media outlets that exercise broad influence, should have a clear picture of what school parents think and how deeply they care. Do you know what budget proposals exist for your school district? Do you know what the debate is about? Is your perspective and that of like-minded parents being expressed? Are you being heard?

• •

Relevant Facts

Average annual expenditure per pupil in public K–12 enrollment: $6,251

Government funding of public education as percent of total K–12:

> Federal: 6.9 percent
> State: 51.1 percent
> Local: 42 percent

• •

Education policy. Whereas schools are administered locally, they can be significantly impacted by policies which originate at the state and federal level.

Areas where this occurs include: standardized testing, mandated by state and federal government; school choice, which in some places means the ability to attend a public school other than your neighborhood school yet elsewhere serves as the code phrase for school voucher proposals; fairness in school-by-school spending, with states grappling for ways to diminish inequities between schools.

Policies formulated at such distance from your school are predictably less sensitive to your viewpoint. Ironically, it is precisely these policies which are asserting an ever greater influence on the day-to-to-day activities of your child's schooling.

Do you know what the impact will be of state and federal proposals regarding public education? Can you trace the line extending from that distant point on Capitol Hill to your child's classroom? If not, the NEA, the PTA, and local pro-public school activists will be happy to help you learn.

....

Coon Rapids, Minnesota: Getting off the Fence

Carol Lowery's involvement in her child's school began quite slowly, without a hint of the consuming passion it would become.

When her children—she has three—were in their early grades at Sand Creek Elementary, Carol managed to work full-time in marketing. Gradually, as the children's individual school needs mounted, principally in the area of homework, Carol made the decision to make herself more available and, knowing her family could still make it financially, she decided to cut back to part-time work.

If she had a spare hour or two, she'd go to the school to help the teacher with a project. She found that she loved the feeling of passing by her children's classrooms and "seeing their big smiles when they see me." But her involvement was still limited; she had never even attended a PTO meeting.

Then came the referendum levy battle in the fall of 2001. Anoka-Hennepin, a growing district in metropolitan Minneapolis with 48,000 students, has been faced in recent years with the twin problem of an expanding school population and intensifying taxpayer frugality.

The goal of the levy was to raise additional funds for the purpose of: achieving smaller class sizes; restoring teacher positions that had been recently cut; supporting teacher training explicitly to improve methods for addressing the individual needs of underchallenged and struggling students; and upgrading and integrating computer technology.

In sum, the levy funds were earmarked for programs and positions that are key to improved education.

The levy would raise an additional $28.35 million in 2002, an increased allocation of approximately $590 per student. The means of raising this money would principally be through property taxes, although changes made in the state property tax assessments would lessen by about half the total cost to the average homeowner.

Carol Lowery did the math, looked at the benefits, and had not a flicker of confusion about the right way to vote. Moreover, she could see no reason why any parent, or conscientious citizen for that matter, would oppose the referendum. "I became less passive. These are my kids," Carol explains of that pivotal realization. "I got off the fence."

In getting "off the fence," Carol was lucky to be guided by the Anoka-Hennepin School District's official, paid Parent Involvement Coordinator, Linda Rodgers. "Providing families with the tools to succeed" is how the district describes the mission of its ambitious ten-year-old program, which includes everything from homework workshops to support groups to legislative lobbying.

Having a full-time staff person assigned to direct and coordinate parent activities is, in Rodgers' words, "critical." The district has some 8,000 parent or guardian volunteers who contribute an estimated one million dollars in work to the schools every year. Rodgers' role is also critical to the political outreach a school district needs to pass a levy referendum in a tough economic climate.

Part of Rodgers' job is to cultivate parent-activists within the community. Carol Lowery was quickly identified, Rodgers jocularly noted, as "a talented rookie." As the November 6 levy vote approached, with all its vital consequences for education within the district, Carol joined two other parents in heading the get-out-the-vote effort.

Carol approached this task with astonishing zeal. She helped write and design pro-referendum brochures that were mailed to district residents. She handed out flyers at high school football games and at Anoka's celebrated Halloween parade. She enlisted parents to hand out, along with Halloween candy, book markers listing the top ten reasons to vote for the levy ("9. Retro fashion may be in style—retro textbooks are not. 10. Standing room only in a concert hall defines success; in a classroom it's a failure").

"I'd never had a passion before," Carol says of the long hours she poured into the campaign.

The levy was far from unopposed. The Minnesota Taxpayers League, generally unfriendly to any tax increase, waged a determined counteroffensive, purchasing large amounts of media time in the Twin Cities area. In addition, widely publicized remarks critical of school spending made by Jesse Ventura, the state's governor, served to fuel anti-levy sentiment.

A close vote was widely predicted. Carol was optimistic. After all, she reasoned, why wouldn't a community respond positively to the urgent needs of so cherished an institution as its schools?

Likewise, Linda Rodgers felt that her years of outreach would result in a favorable vote. One of her theories has been that public schools can best be understood as living organisms that require many points of contact with their environment in order to thrive. Schools, like cellular creatures, need to constantly learn how to respond and adapt. "The more schools interact with the community," Rodgers contends, "the more highly valued and supported they will be."

On November 6, 2001, the referendum levy was narrowly defeated by Anoka-Hennepin voters. Carol was upset. A much-needed proposal had been rejected. The consequences, she feared, would be immediate (there was talk of cutting bus service and abandoning music and language for elementary students) and personal. After all, this was about her children's future. There was no silver lining that she could see.

But I see one in Carol's concluding remark: "I feel I've signed on for the duration of my children's schooling," Carol reflects. "The more involved I get, the more I see that I can't run away."

Are There Groups to Join?

Most schools have either a formal or informal parents group that can be a source of excellent insight and advice as you navigate through public school. Needless to say, volunteers are welcome.

The best known parent organization, and the one you're most likely to run into at your child's school, is the Parent-Teacher Association (PTA). The group has 6.5 million members and was founded in 1897. In the words of Shirley Igo, president of the national PTA, "We believe that parents should be completely involved and should be a full partner, along with teachers, in their child's education."

The PTA is active on all levels of schooling, from school site councils to federal and state legislation that affects education. They advocate parent participation on curriculum and discipline policy committees, search committees for superintendents and principals, and school site councils. "Parents and schools need to be in synch," says Igo.

Other parent groups are emerging, perhaps in response to the increasingly embattled place of public schools in some communities. One such organization worth your attention is Parents for Public Schools (PPS), which was formed in Jackson, Mississippi, in 1989, and now has chapters in fifteen states.

Founded by Kelly Alin Butler to mobilize parents tempted to send their children to private school, PPS has become a staunch advocate for parent involvement. PPS stresses that parents should demonstrate "a posture of ownership" toward the school and take a meaningful role in important decisions about running it. This can take the form of conducting school tours for parents to advising the school district about parent involvement issues. "Public education," declares Butler, "is integral to democracy."

The Big Picture

The research evidence is beyond dispute. When schools work together with families to support learning, very good things happen: student attitudes, attendance, homework, and report cards improve.

A study recently released by the U.S. Department of Education showed that the reading and math scores of low-achieving students rose 40 to 50 percent between third and fifth grade when teachers reached out to families, and not just when the child was in trouble. I emphasize the research data because parent involvement is sometimes viewed as primarily a feel-good gesture by schools, more public relations than substance. But it's clear that there's more to it. Parent involvement upgrades the essential bottom line—your child's learning. It's that simple.

As I travel the country and visit schools, I have been struck by how almost everyone pays lip service to parent and family involvement, but few seriously apply themselves to making it happen. Why is this?

So much progress has been made in recent years in other areas of school reform—reductions in class size, establishment of challenging academic standards, increase in after-school reading and math programs—why not in parent and family involvement?

I have come to the conclusion that family participation at some level, at any level, at *many* levels, cannot be an afterthought. Schools must take a proactive approach. We must develop innovative ways to reach out and include parents in the mix. Schools should consider the creation of a new position— learning partnership specialist—to explicitly help teachers and staff work with families.

How we get there is open for discussion. Joyce Epstein, director of the National Network of Partnership Schools at the Johns Hopkins University, contends that fostering parent involvement, and channeling it, is "as much the school's responsibility as the reading or math program is its responsibility."

I agree. But for the time being, much of the burden will fall— no surprise—on you. I can't tell you how or when or to what extent to get involved. Such decisions are highly individual.

What I can point out is that schools are a classic demonstration of how individual interests invariably coincide with those of your neighbors and the community surrounding you. True, there are some sectors of our society where it's possible to fulfill personal ambitions with no appreciable improvement occurring to those around you (I think of the acclaimed home run champion whose team invariably loses). But schools are not such a place.

Nor do we want schools to be such a place. We want schools to showcase our national values as well as teach them. Contributing time and effort to a worthy common purpose happens to be one of those values. A pivotal one.

Since the terrorism of last September 11th, there has been a great and welcome upsurge of enthusiasm in America for participation in civic projects that benefit our larger community. *Connections* to each other and to our shared goals—that's what Americans are seeking. Commentators and public figures have clamored to identify good causes that can connect people amidst this newfound spirit of national unity.

Such a public embrace of common purpose represents the America I most cherish. Having spent virtually my entire career in public education, I feel fortunate not to have to look very hard for a connection between my deepest personal concerns and our vital need to prepare children for tomorrow's difficult challenges.

You, the new public school parent, are similarly connected. The schoolhouse door your child enters opens into a world where you too can make a difference.

WEBSITES

National Education Association *www.nea.org*
Parent Teachers Assocation *www.pta.org*
Parents for Public Schools *www.parents4publicschool.com*
Commonwealth Institute for Parent Leadership *www.cipl.org*
Family Education *www.familyeducation.com*

Appendix

Samples of Educational Forms

"Written Prior Notice" Sample

Student: _____ DOB: _____ Meeting Date: _____

WRITTEN PRIOR NOTICE

1. Action which is proposed by the PPT: □ Conduct an Initial Evaluation   □ Conduct a Reevaluation   □ Implement IEP dated: _____

□ Revise IEP dated: _____   □ Determine that student is not eligible for Sp. Ed. /Related Services   □ Determine that student is eligible for Sp. Ed. /Related Services

□ Placement: (specify) _____   □ Discontinue services: (specify) _____   □ Exit from Special Education

□ Other: (specify) _____

Action which is refused by the PPT: □ NA, no action(s) refused by the PPT   □ Action(s) refused: (specify) _____

_____

2. Reasons why the PPT made this decision: □ Evaluation results support action recommended   □ Educational performance supports action recommended

□ Previous IEP goals and objectives have been satisfactorily achieved   □ Student has met Exit Criteria in IEP   □ Other: (specify) _____

_____

3. Other options which the PPT considered and rejected in favor of the decision made: □ Full-time placement in general education with supplementary aids and services (e.g.

resource room, itinerant instruction)   □ No other options were considered and rejected   □ Options considered and rejected: (specify) _____

4. Reason(s) why the PPT rejected these other options (3 above):   □ NA, no other options were considered and rejected   □ Options would not provide student with an appropriate

program in the Least Restrictive Environment   □ Other: (specify) _____

_____

5. Describe any Evaluation Procedures, Tests, Records or Reports the PPT used as a basis for its decision: □ Report Card(s)   □ Teacher Reports   □ Review of Records

□ Cognitive: (dated) _____   □ Classroom Observation: (dated) _____   □ Health/Med.: (dated) _____   □ Motor: (dated) _____

□ Communication: (dated) _____   □ Achievement: (dated) _____   □ Social/Emotional/Behavioral: (dated) _____

□ Developmental: (dated) _____   □ Adaptive: (dated) _____   □ Other: (specify) _____

6. Describe any other factors that are relevant to the PPT's decision: □ Information/concerns shared by parents   □ Information/preferences shared by the student

□ There are no other factors that are relevant to the PPT decision   □ Other: (specify) _____

_____

_____

Parents please note: You have protections under the procedural safeguards of the Individuals with Disabilities Education Act (IDEA). A copy of Procedural Safeguards in Special Education which explains these protections [□ **was made available at the meeting**   □ **is enclosed with this document**]. If you need assistance in understanding the provisions of IDEA, please contact the special education supervisor, your child's principal or the district's special education director.

'Cumulative File,   Parent,   'Supv., Spec. Educ.

2

"Level of Education Performance" Form

Student: _____ DOB: _____ Meeting Date: _____

INDIVIDUALIZED EDUCATION PROGRAM

PRESENT LEVELS OF EDUCATIONAL PERFORMANCE

Classroom Performance/Parent Reports/Assessment Results	Strengths	Concerns/Needs
1. Health & Development (Including Vision/Hearing): ☐ Typical ☐ Other: (specify)		
2. Academic/Cognitive:		
3. Social/Emotional/Behavioral: ☐ Age/grade appropriate ☐ Other: (specify)		
4. Motor: ☐ Age appropriate ☐ Other: (specify)		
5. Communication: ☐ Age appropriate ☐ Other: (specify)		
6. Activities of Daily Living: ☐ Age appropriate ☐ Other: (specify)		
7. Vocational: ☐ NA due to age ☐ Other: (specify)		

8. Describe how the student's disability affects her/his involvement and progress in the general curriculum or participation in appropriate preschool activities:

9. Is the student eligible for special education services?   ☐ Yes   ☐ No

White/Cumulative File, Yellow/Parent, Pink/Supv. Spec. Educ.

3

"Placement Summary" Form

Student: _____ DOB: _____ Meeting Date: _____

INDIVIDUALIZED EDUCATION PROGRAM

PLACEMENT SUMMARY

1. **Placement:**

   ☐ Public School In-District ☐ Separate Sp. Ed. School In-District ☐ Other Public School District ☐ RESC ☐ Private ☐ State Facility

   ☐ Quasi-Public School* ☐ Hospital ☐ Charter School ☐ Homebound ☐ Other: (specify

   ☐ For educational reasons ☐ For non-educational reasons

2. If a residential placement, placement is: ☐ NA (not a residential placement)

3. Justification for removal from Regular Education: *(Note: The LRE Checklist should be used to ensure that procedures related to LRE decision-making are followed.)*

   ☐ Not applicable - Implementation of the student's IEP, with supplementary aids and services, does not require removal from Regular Education.

   ☐ The student cannot receive an appropriate educational program in the regular classroom, even with the use of supplementary aids and services, whereas an appropriate program can be provided in the more restrictive setting being proposed by the PPT.

   ☐ The student's behavior in a regular classroom, even with the use of supplementary aids and services is disruptive to such an extent that it interferes with the ability of the district to make a safe and orderly instructional environment available to students.

   ☐ The student will not receive any significant nonacademic benefit from interacting with nondisabled students.

   ☐ Other: _____

4. **Explanation of the extent, if any, to which the student will not participate with nondisabled students in the regular class and in extracurricular and other nonacademic activities:** ☐ Student will participate fully ☐ Other: (specify) _____

5. **Hours per week the student will spend with nondisabled students:** _____ Hrs.

6. **Exit Criteria:** (Check One)

   ☐ Ability to succeed in Regular Education without Special Education support ☐ Graduation ☐ Age 21 ☐ Other: (specify) _____

7. **Student's projected graduation date is:** _____ (Applies only to students In grades eight through twelve) ☐ NA

8. **Procedures which will be utilized to ensure that the student's parents are regularly Informed of the student's progress toward the annual goals in this IEP and the extent to which that progress is sufficient to enable the student to achieve these IEP Goals by the end of the year** ☐ A report of progress toward the Measurable Annual Goals and Short Term Objectives included in this IEP will be sent to parents as often the district reports progress to parents of students who do not have disabilities. ☐

   Other: (Specify) _____

* *Gilbert School, Norwich Free Academy, Woodstock Academy*

   'Cumulative File, 'Parent, Supv., Spec. Educ.

"Modification and Adaptations" Form

Student: _____ DOB: _____   Meeting Data: _____

INDIVIDUALIZED EDUCATION PROGRAM

MODIFICATIONS/ADAPTATIONS IN REGULAR EDUCATION - INCLUDING NONACADEMIC AND EXTRACURRICULAR ACTIVITIES - AND COLLABORATION/SUPPORTS FOR SCHOOL PERSONNEL

Modifications/Adaptations in Regular Education - Including Nonacademic and Extracurricular Activities	Sites/Activities Where Required and Duration	Required Supports for Personnel and Frequency and Duration of Supports.
Materials/Books/Equipment: ☐ Alternative Text ☐ Consumable Workbook ☐ Modified Worksheets ☐ Manipulatives ☐ Access to Computer ☐ Tape Recorder ☐ Supplementary Visuals ☐ Large Print Text ☐ Spell Check ☐ Calculator ☐ Assistive Technology: (specify) ☐ Other: (specify)		
Tests/Quizzes/Time: ☐ Prior Notice of Tests ☐ Preview Test Procedures ☐ Test Study Guide ☐ Simplify Test Wording ☐ Oral Testing ☐ Limited Multiple Choice ☐ Student Write on Test ☐ Shortened Tasks ☐ Hands-on Projects ☐ Reduced Reading ☐ Alternative Tests ☐ Objective Tests ☐ Extra Credit Options ☐ Extra Time-Written Work ☐ Extra Time-Tests ☐ Extra Time-Projects ☐ Extra Response Time ☐ Pace Long Term Projects ☐ Rephrase Test Questions/Directions ☐ Other: (specify)		
Grading: ☐ No Spelling Penalty ☐ No Handwriting Penalty ☐ Grade Effort + Work ☐ Pass/Fail ☐ Base Grade on IEP ☐ Other: (specify)		
Organization: ☐ Provide Study Outlines ☐ Desktop List of Tasks ☐ List Sequential Steps ☐ Post Routines ☐ Post Assignments ☐ Give One Paper at a Time ☐ Folders to Hold Work ☐ Pencil Box for Tools ☐ Pocket Folder for Work ☐ Assignment Pad ☐ Daily Assignment List ☐ Daily Homework List ☐ Worksheet Formats ☐ Extra Space for Work ☐ Assign Partner ☐ Other: (specify)		
Environment: ☐ Preferential Seating ☐ Clear Work Area ☐ Study Carrel ☐ Other: (specify)		
Behavior Management/Support: ☐ Daily Feedback to Student ☐ Chart Progress ☐ Behavior Contracts ☐ Parent/Guardian Sign Homework ☐ Have Student Restate Information ☐ Positive Reinforcement ☐ Collect Baseline Data ☐ Self/Post Class Rules ☐ Parent/Guardian Sign Behavioral Chart ☐ Provide Lecture Notes/Outline to Student ☐ Cue Expected Behavior ☐ Structure Transitions ☐ Break Between Tasks ☐ Time Out from Positive Reinforcement ☐ Computer Assisted Instruction ☐ Proximity/Touch Control ☐ Contingency Plan ☐ Other: (specify) ☐ Support Auditory Presentations with Visuals		
Instructional Strategies: ☐ Check Work in Progress ☐ Immediate Feedback ☐ Pre-teach Content ☐ Parent/Guardian Sign Homework ☐ Display Key Vocabulary ☐ Extra Drill/Practice ☐ Review Sessions ☐ Review Directions ☐ Provide Student With Vocabulary Word Bank ☐ Use Manipulatives ☐ Modified Content ☐ Assign Study Partner ☐ Personalized Examples ☐ Monitor Assignments ☐ Provide Models ☐ Repeat Instructions ☐ Multi-Sensory Approach ☐ Highlight Key Words ☐ Oral Reminders ☐ Visual Reinforcement ☐ Pictures/Charts ☐ Visual Reminders ☐ Mimed Clues/Gestures ☐ Concrete Examples ☐ Use Mnemonics ☐ Number Line ☐ Other: (specify)		

8

Note: *When specifying required supports for personnel to implement this IEP, include the specific supports required, how often they are to be provided (frequency) and for how long (duration).* (e.g., "the speech/language pathologist will meet with the student's classroom teacher for 20 minutes each week, for the school year, to plan language activities which can be used in the classroom.")

White/Cumulative File, Yellow/Parent, Pink/Supv., Spec. Educ.

<u>Parent/School PARTNERSHIP CONFERENCING QUESTIONNAIRE</u>

Child's Name_____ Date:_____

Parent(s) _____

Since you are your child's first and best teacher, we would like your perceptions of your child as a learner.

Thank you for your help!

1.   Tell us something nice about your child._____
_____
_____
_____

2.   What does your child like to do outside of school?_____
_____
_____
_____

3.   What are your child's talents (art, music, etc.)?_____
_____
_____
_____

4.   List some of your child's strengths at school and challenges at school._____
_____
_____
_____

5.   What are some goals for your child this year?
     Academic: Social:

     _____   _____
     _____   _____
     _____   _____

6.   What is the most important thing you, as a parent, do for your child to support his/her learning?_____
_____
_____
_____
_____

Over . . . .

7. What things might your child worry about?_____ . _____
_____
_____
_____

8. Are there any talents/skills **you** would be willing to share with the class (sewing, arts, crafts, careers, culture, etc.)?_____
_____
_____
_____

9. What family activities do you enjoy doing together?_____
_____
_____
_____

10. Do you read together regularly? If so, how often and what kinds of books do you enjoy?_
_____
_____
_____

11. Is there any other information that would be helpful to the classroom teacher?_____
_____
_____
_____

Thank you for taking the time to share with me about your child.

Sincerely,

Parent's name_____
Address_____
Home phone_____ **Work phone**_____
Best time to be contacted_____

Index

teachers (*cont.*)
  selection of, 10–11, 25–28
  standardized tests and, 120–22, 127
  substitute, 17–22, 28–29
  and underchallenged student, 59–61
team teaching, 246
teasing, 188
  see also bullying and harassment
technology, 134–35
  facts about, 136
  learning and, 131, 132–33, 136, 146–47
  practices to avoid with, 140–41
  see also computers
terms, "EduSpeak," 241–46
Test of Auditory Perceptual Skills (TAPS), 167
tests:
  classroom, 110
  computers and, 132, 141–42
  diagnostic, 111
  I.Q., 111, 241
  pretests, 56–57, 66, 67
  special education assessment, 48, 166–68, 171, 180
tests, standardized, 109–29, 232
  ability (aptitude), 241
  achievement, 241–42
  child's understanding of importance of, 114
  criterion-referenced, 111, 115, 116
  curriculum and, 123–24, 127
  defined, 110
  disabilities and, 126
  flaws of, 119–20, 121
  goals of, 113–14
  high-stakes, 110, 111, 125, 128, 241–42

  importance of, 126–27
  norm-referenced, 111, 112, 115, 116, 119
  performance assessments, 111–12
  poll on, 126
  portfolio assessments, 112
  preparation for, 124–25
  school quality and, 120–21
  teaching to, 121–22
  types of, 110–12
  use of results of, 114–15
  what results reveal, 115–16
  what to expect, 112–13
thinking skills, 249
tiered assignments, 62
tracking, 62, 68–69, 246
tutoring, 42, 70

violence, 202–3, 204, 206, 232
  see also bullying and harassment
visual perception difficulty, 169
volunteering, 159, 160
vouchers, 223, 224, 228–29, 245, 246

websites:
  for disabilities, 184–85
  for gifted children, 76
  for homework, 93
  for math, reading, and learning, 222
  for parent involvement, 262
  of schools, 7
  for school safety, 206
  for technology in education, 148
Weschsler Intelligence Score of Children (WISC), 167, 171
whole language, 246
Woodcock Johnson test, 167, 171